Contents

Young People in Foster and Residential Care

Answers to questions you may be asked

by 11-18 year olds in your care

Ann Wheal

Russell House Publishing

Young people in foster and residential care

Answers to questions you may be asked by 11-18 year olds in your care

This is an expanded and updated third edition of a book originally called *Answers for Carers* (Longman 1994; Pavilion 1999), published in 2003 by:

Russell House Publishing Ltd.

4 St. George's House

Uplyme Road

Lyme Regis

Dorset DT7 3LS

Tel: 01297-443948

Fax: 01297-442722

e-mail: help@russellhouse.co.uk

www.russellhouse.co.uk

British Library Cataloguing-in-publication Data:

A catalogue record for this book is available from the British Library.

ISBN: 1-903855-27-6

Design and layout by Jeremy Spencer. Cover illustration by Hemera.

Printed by Cromwell Press, Trowbridge.

About Russell House Publishing

RHP is a group of social work, probation, education and youth and community work practitioners and academics working in collaboration with a professional publishing team.

Our aim is to work closely with the field to produce innovative and valuable materials to help managers, trainers, practitioners and students. We are keen to receive feedback on publications and new ideas for future projects.

For details of our other publications please visit our website or ask us for a catalogue. Contact details are on this page.

About this book

Who is the book for?

This handbook has been produced for:

- Residential and foster carers in the United Kingdom.

- Carers working with young people with disabilities.

- Those working with young people who have left, or who will shortly be leaving care.

How the book works

This book has been developed:

- For young people and carers to read together.

- To provide **carers** with answers to questions they may have about bringing up a young person aged 11-18.

 What can the carer do to help young people settle?

- To help carers answer the many questions a **young person** aged 11-18 may ask about their time being looked after and when they leave 'care'.

 What's happening to me?

- To be used as a 'talking tool' when carers are working in partnership with young people, either in groups or one-to-one. In this way it is hoped young people will learn to take responsibility for their own future.

The book may be used as a way to start talking with young people about issues that extend beyond the home.

A number of pages have questions a young person might ask, along with some suggested answers.

Checklists and extra information that will only be of interest to particular young people at particular times have also been included. These have been written as though they are for the young person and may be photocopied without permission.

No mention has been made of benefits entitlement as these vary with individual circumstances.

This handbook has been written so that it may also be useful for those being assessed for NVQ (SNVQ) qualifications and for those undertaking childcare placements as part of their qualifying or post qualifying courses.

The Children Act (1991), the Children (Scotland) Act (1995) and the Children's Order (Northern Ireland) (1995) were designed to:

- Encourage carers to work in partnership with the young people in their care.

- Encourage young people to return to their parents home as soon as possible, if appropriate.

- Encourage those looking after the young people to work with them in all sorts of ways, so that these young people will be able to take their place in society in the future.

This book will seek to ensure that there is no unfair discrimination on the grounds of age, gender, disability (including use of sign language), race, ethnic origin, nationality, sexual orientation, social class, religion or language.

What readers said about previous editions of this book

Answers is great, I use it all the time.

Ena Fry, Fostering Network

We welcome the publication. It is informative, accessible, and easy to use and provides vital information about young people's rights and responsibilities.

BAAF (British Association for Adoption and Fostering)

...a very good handbook for new foster carers, full of useful information and easy to understand (the best yet!).

Foster carer

I was particularly impressed that there is a distinct lack of jargon. It certainly made the introduction of our latest foster child very easy.

Foster carer

Use of the handbook was very good as a back up to what I had already explained to the client. I could then show the client and they could read it easily to confirm my decision. Open discussions amongst the children are great. They can air their grievances etc. which can help a sometimes explosive situation. Involving the clients builds up interest, self-esteem etc. – very good.

Care assistant

...extremely useful for in-house training for staff, residents, foster carers and clients; supervision with staff and residents; staff meetings and residents' meetings; a quick reference for service users, families and friends. Available for residents, families, friends and community.

Residential carer

I found this handbook excellent, the most informative information I've ever received, both for myself and the young people I care for.

Foster carer

...very useful for NVQ (SNVQ) and social care related courses.

Residential manager

A book like this could ensure that all staff have some training, whatever the level they are employed at.

Student

Answers is brilliant.

Family resource centre manager

Acknowledgements

In 1992 the Department of Social Work Studies at the University of Southampton took part in a research project which became known as the Dolphin Project. During the project, Daphne Walder and I met young people who were being looked after in Birmingham, Berkshire and Hampshire. They told us what they knew about the Children Act and also about their time in children's homes and in foster care. Ann Buchanan also met their carers.

A report called *Answering Back: A Young Person's View of the Children Act* was published. *Answers for Carers* was one of the many outcomes of this report.

There is a similar book for carers of children under 11 years entitled *The Foster Carer's Handbook* by Ann Wheal, published by Russell House Publishing.

Many people helped in so many ways with the previous editions by assisting with funding; being members of our working party; acting as critical readers; advisers and evaluators and the young people themselves who made suggestions and criticisms very willingly. I am extremely grateful to each and every one of them for their valued contribution.

I would particularly like to thank Ann Buchanan who was deeply involved in the first edition of this book and without whom I would probably not have started writing in the first place.

For help with this edition I would like to thank Sue Daniel, Sue Smith, Sue Blundell, Ena Fry and, of course, my husband for his patience, tolerance and love.

The updating of this manuscript has been carried out using information contained in a variety of web sites, Fostering Network's information leaflets, details received from the Scottish Throughcare and Aftercare Service, and information contained in *Rostrum, The Voice of Social Work in Scotland*, published by BASW.

Ann Wheal
2003

Section 1
Who cares?

Introduction: inch by inch - setting up young people to succeed

This book is about rights and responsibilities.

- What exactly do we mean?

- Whose rights?

- Whose responsibilities? The young person's, or the carer's?

The answer is **both**. By using this book as a guide we hope you will work with the young people in your care, explaining to them:

- Exactly what their rights are.

- How important it is to use these rights.

- How to use these rights responsibly.

The more information young people have, the better equipped they will be to make decisions that affect their lives. This doesn't happen overnight. They need to be taught skills to help them make these decisions and when these decisions turn out to be wrong, to know how to pick up the pieces and start again, no matter how painful it is.

He who has never made a mistake, has never made anything.

This old saying is true of us all, and the young people in your care need your time and patience, as well as all the information you can give them, to help them make informed choices and sensible decisions about their lives. Some people may think that if a young person is given too much information it may be abused. Our experience points to the reverse. The more information young people have the better able they are to successfully plan their lives and their future.

Everyone needs to be valued, to feel special, and to feel important. By treating all young people as individuals, working with and caring for them, you will build up their self-esteem.

A good carer is someone who sits down and listens to you and discusses things with you.

Young person's view

Carers' responsibilities

A carer should be able to:

- Provide each young person with food, clothing, a bed and a small personal area, or separate room if possible.
- Include each young person in the activities of the home.
- Establish clear expectations and limits.
- Discipline fairly.
- Deal with negative behaviour in a positive way.
- Reward good behaviour.
- Promote and encourage a relationship with the birth family.
- Encourage a young person's cultural and religious heritage and behave in a way which does not discriminate.
- Arrange for routine, and emergency, medical and dental care.
- Assume responsibility for the young person's daily school activities and educational needs.
- Promote a young person's self-esteem and positive self-image.
- Respect the young person and their birth family.
- Work with all concerned, including the young person, to make a permanent plan for them.
- Help prepare the young person to return to their birth family or be placed with relatives or friends, adoptive parents, or to live independently.
- Help the young person to speak up, to be heard and to be listened to.
- To listen, to understand and to relate to each young person.

There may be others you think should be added to this list.

Young people want their carers to:

- Share information with the young person about their rights under the law and make sure that the young person fully understands any legal order affecting them.
- Acknowledge difference whether due to racial origin, language, religion or culture; respect and support young people and challenge discrimination.
- Provide opportunities for young people to make choices and to learn about making decisions; involve them in planning.
- Remember that in dealing with parents, young people are also partners in the decision-making and may need support in making their views known.
- Help young people to participate in their reviews.
- Prepare young people for independence.
- Share information about pocket money and allowances.
- Support young people in making a complaint.
- Help young people develop other relationships, other partnerships.
- Advocate for young people in obtaining equal opportunity in education.
- Recognise and support young people in distress.
- Recognise that the best partner may be the key residential worker, foster carer or leaving-care worker.

Training for carers

Introduction

A well-trained workforce is desirable in any discipline but with adults working with vulnerable children and young people it is essential.

The lives of children and their families are too important to be left to 'trial and error'. Training can make people more aware of the skills and personal qualities they already have and help develop new skills and awareness. It is an opportunity to communicate the body of knowledge derived from research and practice. Training gives an opportunity to meet with other carers and help them to feel less isolated.

Initial training for carers is mandatory for approved foster carers. Some schemes insist that carers attend other training and many independent fostering agencies (IFAs) also seem to make attendance at training compulsory. The 'voluntary' nature of fostering leads social workers to some times feel that they cannot enforce carers to attend training.

Most new fostering households will have one carer who has attended a preparation course prior to approval. The goal is to have both partners in a two-partner home attend but this often does not happen.

Because fostering is organised locally **post-approval training** varies. Some carers will be offered a good rolling programme, help with transport and childcare and a crèche when necessary. Popular topics for post-approval training are:

- safer caring
- managing behaviour
- contact
- record keeping
- moving children and young people on

Training - general

The *National Standards in Foster Care* (Department of Health, 1999) the government's initiative on training for residential and foster carers and changes in social work training have highlighted the whole question of skills, knowledge, qualities and qualifications required by those caring for children and young people.

The *Looking After Children* (LAC) *assessment and action records* have also provided a powerful impetus for the development of training for carers. These records, which must be completed for every looked-after child, cover:

- health
- education
- identity
- family and social relationships
- social presentation
- emotional and behavioural development
- self-care skills

The NVQ (SNVQ) *Caring for children and young people* award is a nationally recognised qualification for carers and social workers. The approach to this again varies, with some local authorities and IFAs giving all their carers the opportunity to work towards this award, while other carers report a lack of knowledge among social work staff and very little idea as to how to go about achieving the award.

Some colleges offer NVQ courses, but this is a misnomer as the award can only be achieved by being assessed while doing the job. Training can help to provide underpinning knowledge and fill in gaps in the carers' knowledge but without assessment the award cannot be gained.

S/NVQ caring for children and young people

This offers a comprehensive framework of standards for use as a benchmark for practice. The qualification is based around achieving competence at work.

There are some **compulsory units**, titled, for example:

- Promote equality, diversity and rights.
- Contribute to the protection of children from abuse.
- Receive, transmit, store and retrieve information.
- Contribute to the development, provision and review of care programmes.

Optional units cover areas such as:

- health
- education
- identity
- managing change
- working with the child's family
- dealing with challenging behaviour

Training courses

Throughout their time as carers, training should be provided to carers on topics such as:

- counselling
- drug abuse
- HIV/AIDS
- disability
- new legislation

There are also opportunities for carers to take further qualifications and advanced awards.

For further information or training contact:

- Fostering Network.
- Local authority training departments.
- Colleges and universities in your area.
- NCVQ (National Council for Vocational Qualifications) Tel. 020 7387 9898.
- SCOTVEC: Tel. 00 141 248 7900.

Who's who in helping young people?

Helpers for you and the young people in your care

The best helpers are often the young person's family and friends, but the following may also be involved:

Key worker

In residential settings, the **key workers** are responsible for the young people. They build a relationship with the young person, assess the young person's needs, and help to meet those needs. They are involved with admissions; planning; liaising with other agencies and with parents; and for the overall well-being of the young person.

Foster carer

Foster carers have an agreement with a social service, or an IFA (Independent Fostering Agency). The young person lives in the foster carer's own home. There are many different types of foster carers: short term, long term and specialist foster carers, who are trained and have chosen to look after teenagers, young people with disabilities or those with behavioural problems. Foster carers also like to get to know a young person really well and help them in many different ways.

Field social worker

All young people who are being looked after should have a **field social worker** who is based in the local area office from which the young person came. In some areas they are called **care managers**. Generally speaking, their job is to keep in touch with the young person, their family and residential or foster carers, and to make sure plans are carried out. They usually attend planning meetings and reviews, and handle any court matters. The field social worker is the first line of contact for the young person and the residential and foster carer.

Key worker's line manager

This is the person who is responsible for the key worker. Key workers will go to their **line manager** for advice and guidance. This person may be the manager of the home. If a young person has a disagreement with their key worker, they may want to discuss this with another worker or the line manager.

Family placement worker/foster carer's social worker

Most foster carers will have their own social worker who is based in the **Fostering Family Placement office**. This person advises the foster carer about general fostering issues. They are similar to the key worker's line manager.

Team managers/area managers/directors of social services

Most social service departments are organised like pyramids, with **team managers**, **area managers** and **deputy directors** and finally the **director**. Each level is responsible for the level below. It is a good idea to find out how your social services are organised, as occasionally you might need the help of someone very senior.

Other helpers who may be involved

Children's Rights Officer (CRO)

Children's rights are laid down by the UN Convention on the Rights of the Child. Young people in residential and foster care should be able to telephone the **CRO** and discuss in confidence anything that is bothering them.

It is important that children and young people know what their rights are and how they can exercise those rights. This includes their right to challenge decisions and to question the way in which services are provided. This sometimes causes anxiety in some quarters but research shows that where young people are empowered to express their views and are listened to with respect they act responsibly and respect different views. It is where young people are not listened to and feel powerless that they can behave in sometimes irresponsible ways.

Independent visitor

An **independent visitor** may be appointed if it is thought necessary when the first plan for the young person is drawn up; it may also be decided at a review, if the young person concerned agrees.

 Why might a young person need an independent visitor?

They may benefit from someone else coming to visit them if:

- They are not in contact with their parents.
- They hardly ever see their parents.

However, if they are settled in a residential home or foster home and have lots of other friends and visitors, it may not be thought necessary. If it is not possible for a young person to live in a placement with carers of similar background, race or culture then an independent visitor could become a link with their own community. Independent visitors:

- Try to help a young person by advising or befriending them.

- Try to help a young person in their social, emotional, religious or cultural development.

- May advise a young person on any matter they think fit or if the young person asks for help.

- In some situations they may act as an advocate, say where the young person feels they are not being cared for properly or their views are not being listened to or considered. They will try to sort out the situation.

Normally the young person's social worker will have details of the procedure or your manager should be able to help. There will be several 'getting to know you' meetings where both the young person and the visitor can decide whether to go ahead with the arrangement. At all times the young person's best interests and wishes come first.

The visitor may see the young person only for a short while until relationships with the parents improves, or it may go on for several years; it all depends on the circumstances. It will be discussed at every review. Sometimes they will visit the young person, or the young person may go out and meet them 'on neutral ground', or go on a visit. Occasionally the independent visitor may also invite the young person to their own home. This may of course, be subject to certain controls.

 ## Are independent representatives the same?

An **independent representative** (IR) is not the same. An IR is a person who visits young people who are in secure accommodation to ensure they are treated fairly and receive suitable care. They are independent both of the secure unit and of the care authority. They will:

- Visit every young person as soon as possible after admission and regularly afterwards.
- Listen to the young person.
- Tell them their rights.
- Take up matters on behalf of the young person.
- Help them write letters or see an appropriate person.

Advocate

An **advocate** is a volunteer, who speaks up for and on behalf of a young person. They may find out information that a young person needs or they may try to get things changed on behalf of a young person. They may also attend reviews or planning meetings if they are invited by the young person. Much of what they do will be similar to an independent person except that they are not appointed by the local authority but chosen by the young person. Some organisations such as the Voice of the Child in Care (VCC) offer an advocacy service for young people.

Mentor

A **mentor** is a person (often a volunteer) who is available to give one-to-one advice and encouragement during particular periods in a young person's life, such as leaving care. Mentoring seeks to realise and fulfil the potential of a young person, develop their skills and help promote new opportunities for them.

Personal adviser

In England **personal advisers** may be part of the *Connexions* service. However, all young people should have access to a personal adviser whose aim will be to ensure that the needs of individual young people are met so that they are able and motivated to engage in education, training and work opportunities to achieve their full potential.

The personal adviser's role may include any or all of the following elements:

- Engaging with young people to identify and address their needs, offering information, advice and guidance on learning and career options and personal development opportunities, with a view to raising the aspirations of each young person.

- Utilising and supporting education and training institutions and employees in meeting the needs of young people.

- Working with a network of voluntary, statutory and community agencies, and commercial bodies to ensure a coherent approach to support for the young person.

- Working with parents, carers and families to support young people.

- Managing information effectively to facilitate the process of meeting the needs of young people.

Young people leaving care may also have a personal adviser who is part of the leaving care team.

Children's Commissioner

In Wales and Northern Ireland there is a **Children's Commissioner**, and in Scotland it is anticipated that one for Scotland will be appointed shortly. However, although England very much supports the concept of the rights of the child and has implemented different initiatives, so far there are no plans for a Children's Commissioner for England, despite much lobbying for such an appointment.

The Commissioner is a champion for all children and young people but especially for those most at risk of exclusion and deprivation.

The four main areas of work are:

1. Promoting and safeguarding children's rights.
2. Communicating with children.
3. Investigations and complaints.
4. Promoting good practice.

Complaints officer

Every local authority must have a **complaints officer** who is responsible for investigating complaints (see page 23).

Children's guardian (England and Wales) and curator ad litem/ safeguarder (Scotland)

These are people who have a unique opportunity to enquire into the needs of children and young people through contact with parents, family and a wide range of professionals as well as seeking the views of the children and young people themselves. They then write reports for **children's hearings** (safeguarders) and **the courts** (children's guardians and curators ad litem) which are used as part of the decision-making process in deciding what is in the child's best interest.

Education welfare officers

Their job is to be a link between the school and the residential or foster home. **Education welfare officers** talk to the school about any problem a young person may be having at school; for example, bullying. They are also involved when a young person is truanting. They can usually be contacted through the school.

Educational psychologist

If a young person is having real difficulties in learning or concentrating at school, the head teacher may ask for an educational psychologist to see them. An **educational psychologist** is not a psychiatrist, but someone who has special knowledge about how children learn and what may be causing them to have difficulties. Educational psychologists are involved when young people need specific educational help to overcome their difficulties.

Child guidance workers

Child guidance workers help young people who may have an emotional or behavioural problem, in particular because of some earlier unhappy experience. A child psychiatrist will be part of the team which includes psychologists and specialist social workers. With the help of the young person, their carer or their family, the child guidance worker draws up a plan to help overcome the difficulties.

Section 2
Being looked after

Introduction: settling in

When a young person is first looked after by social services the young person will probably have been under considerable strain and stress, so it is very important that this early stage is well planned and handled carefully.

Each young person will be different and will need to be treated differently: they may want, for example:

- To be on their own.

- To talk to you alone.

- To talk to another young person.

- To very quickly become one of the 'gang'.

Quite often they may be rude or aggressive, or even totally silent and not eat. Whatever their reaction in the first few days let them be alone – yet not alone – be alert, watch and observe and be there when needed. Gradually try to persuade them to take part in the life of their new home. Give them a welcoming, warm environment. Explain what is going on, why they are there, and if you know, how long for.

Tell them how the system works, who is responsible for them and who they can go to if they need help. Let them tell you about their previous experience, where they lived and what the rules were. They could make a list, with addresses if possible, in case they need the information later. They could also list their previous schools and the names and addresses of people who are important to them.

 What's happening to me?

The young person in your care may be confused about who's who, and what is happening to them. If they don't know:

- Explain what a social worker does.

- What their court order means if they have one.

- What the many new terms they will hear mean.

It will all help to make them feel more secure and to settle more easily.

What can the carer do to help young people settle?

Your job in the first few days is to help them pick up the pieces of their lives.

Encourage them to:

- Go back to school as soon as possible.
- Make contact with their family (if that's possible) and friends.
- Talk through with you what has happened.
- Talk about what interests them.

They need your help to make sense of what is happening.

Don't be put off if you are rejected at first. Try again. Try a different approach. Gradually they'll come round and want to talk. It may be particularly difficult for young people from different cultures and backgrounds to get their message over.

Meetings

Meetings, meetings, meetings. There are so many different meetings which often seem to be a waste of time. However, meetings are useful for:

- gaining consensus
- sharing views
- obtaining information
- solving problems
- reaching decisions
- making plans
- checking progress

To be effective, meetings need to achieve their aim in a reasonable way in a reasonable time, leaving a trail of **clear crisp decisions**.

Planning your meeting

Successful meetings depend upon good planning. Detailed plans need to be made before the meeting – who needs to attend and what preparation they need to do before taking part. This matters as much as the conduct of the meeting itself. It is a good idea to go over review forms or details of the meeting with the young person beforehand. Talk about what questions they may want to ask and the best way to do so. Let them know that their contribution will be welcome and valued. Young people are much more likely to attend the meeting if they can see its purpose and feel it will be worthwhile.

The following should help whoever is organising the meeting. Items marked with a * apply to whoever is chairing the meeting.

Time and date

If the meeting is a planning or review meeting then it should be arranged so that the young person can easily attend. Always try to set the date for the next meeting before closing the present meeting if this is possible.

Place

Choose a venue that is suitable for the occasion and prepare well before the meeting begins, so that if anyone arrives early they have somewhere to go. You may want to think about the following:

- How should the chairs and, if needed, any tables be laid out?
- Would comfortable chairs and coffee tables be better?
- What equipment is needed e.g. tape recorder, flip chart?
- Does the meeting need to be on neutral ground?
- Is the environment pleasant and suitable for the occasion?
- Is access easy?
- Is there parking available or is there public transport close by?
- Will anyone require transport or their expenses paid in advance?

Agenda

This should be prepared and, if possible, published beforehand. It should identify the topics to be considered, and also, who is to introduce the subject.*

Points you might consider:

- It is more important to examine the future than to go back over the past.
- Don't have too many items. A long agenda is tiring and boring and items will not get the attention they deserve.
- If the meeting is informal, let those present know what you want to discuss before you begin.

Time-keeping

- A prompt start makes good use of the time available. Any delay in starting encourages people to arrive late in the future.
- Breaks are useful to divide up different topics and prevent boredom. If you are chairing the meeting do control the length of breaks and keep pressure up on progress.*
- Set a finish time and keep to it. Say what it will be at the beginning of the meeting. We owe it to other people to make the best use of their time.*
- Announce (approximately 10 minutes before the end of the meeting) that the meeting is drawing to a close.*

Minutes, notes

Unfortunately, minutes are often used as a form of protection or insurance. They therefore contain a lot about 'who said what'. The importance of minutes is that they record decisions reached and actions planned. In other words, who is to do what and by when?

Size of meetings

The meeting needs to be manageable. Large meetings prevent full contributions and become more formal. Small meetings have limited expertise, but are less formal. One way of keeping attendance to a reasonable number is to have people attend solely for the items which concern them.

The meeting

The carer should help to ensure the young person sits in a suitable place. If the young person wishes, you should sit next to them. Be prepared! Have ready some:

- Ideas to encourage the young person to suggest solutions if possible.
- Strategies to help the young person say what they think.

Would providing tea or coffee help the meeting or would it be a distraction? Plan accordingly.

End of the meeting

- Make sure the meeting ends with a positive feeling and clearly agreed aims and objectives.*
- Summarise what has taken place.*
- Who will do what and by when.*
- Set the date for the next meeting.*
- Finish on time.

Planning meetings

Every young person must have an up-to-date plan so that they know where they stand and what it is hoped will happen to them in the future. They should take part in making this plan which will then have their commitment. In some cases an interpreter may be needed. Your local authority will give you guidance on this. Sometimes the first planning meeting takes place before the young person leaves home but, if not, as soon as possible afterwards.

 What will be on the plan?

- What the young person's needs are, including health, diet, religion, language, education, friends, and carers. This may mean finding out where particular shops – selling, for example, African Caribbean food or Asian cosmetics – are located.
- If a young person is disabled, what extra help they need.
- Where the young person will be living.
- If it is possible to predict how long they are likely to be looked after by social services.
- What will happen in the future, and when it will happen.
- When the young person will see their parents, and how the parents will be involved.
- What will happen if things don't work out as planned.
- Arrangements for education and health care.
- Who is responsible for carrying out the plan.

Who goes to a planning meeting?

Whenever possible:

- the young person
- parents
- the social worker
- anyone else who cares about the young person such as grandparents, aunts, uncles, friends
- anyone who works with the young person, such as the manager of a children's home
- foster carer/key worker
- other people may be invited such as teachers, doctors, educational welfare officers etc.

Reviews

Lots of young people will say reviews are a waste of time but reviews are very important for young people, even though quite often they don't realise it. They should be encouraged to attend whenever possible and if they can't attend, to send their apologies and any comments they may have. Whoever is responsible for organising a young person's review should make sure that the time and place is suitable for everyone especially the young person. It is after all their review.

A young person can if they wish ask for a review to take place.

What are reviews?

Reviews are regular meetings which social services must hold for all young people who are looked after by them. A review is held:

- To make sure that the plans made for the young person are being carried out.
- To decide whether the plans should be changed in any way.

How often do they happen?

They are held within four weeks of when a young person is first looked after, but they may be held earlier; then within three months; then within six months. If a lot is happening or there is a problem, then reviews may be held more often.

Must I go to them?

It's a very good idea for the young person to attend as they can have their say about what's going on. Encourage the young person to speak up for themselves, to moan or make suggestions. The young person can take a friend or someone else they trust and can also get that person to speak on their behalf if they find talking in front of everyone difficult. If it really isn't possible for the young person to attend their review, they can write down what they want to say and ask someone else to read it for them.

 ## Who will be there?

All the people who are concerned about the young person should be there including their parents, carer, social worker and sometimes teacher and/or interpreter. If, at the review, the young person doesn't want to say what they feel in front of their parents they can ask for them to leave the room. The parents might also ask for the young person to leave the room whilst they have their say. If it is known that this might happen it is a good idea to tell either the young person or the parents in advance.

 ## What happens before the review?

The young person will be asked, usually to write down, sometimes on a printed form:

- How they are getting on.
- What they want to happen in the future.
- Anything else they would like to talk about at the review.

Their social worker and carer will also be asked to write down what they think as well. Everyone should see what the others have written before the review.

 ## Will someone take notes of what is said at the meeting?

Yes, and everyone including the young person should get a copy. If a young person is not happy they should tell you or their social worker. If they feel strongly, encourage them to put their view in writing of what happened, and try to get the notes changed. It's a good idea for the young person to keep their own notes of what happened anyway or to write down the main points afterwards.

Help them to follow up matters, if what has been agreed doesn't happen within a reasonable amount of time. The time for something to happen or for action to be taken should be agreed at the review.

Child protection conference and register

 ## What is a child protection conference?

This is a meeting that is called if either social services, the police, a teacher or someone from the health service, such as a doctor, thinks a young person may be suffering, or at serious risk of suffering, a significant harm, and may need protection, because of:

- physical injury
- neglect
- sexual abuse
- emotional abuse

 ## Who goes to a child protection conference?

Any of the following **may** attend:

- the young person
- the parents
- their social worker and other social services officials
- the police
- a teacher
- a doctor or someone from the health authority
- if the person is 'being looked after' their carer may attend

The young person may also bring along a friend or someone they trust just to be there or to speak on their behalf.

A member of staff from the social services department usually chairs the meeting and a specially trained clerk will be in attendance to take the minutes.

 ## Who gets a copy of the minutes?

Everyone present at the meeting will get a copy. If the parents are only present for part of the time then they will only be given the minutes of that part of the meeting. If there is a period for professionals only, notes of that part of the meeting will be confidential.

What happens at the meeting?

The first Child Protection Conference is called to exchange information and to decide on whether the young person should be placed on the Child Protection Register. If so, then someone will be nominated to:

- Co-ordinate the plan.
- Help the young person and parents to take part in the plan.
- Keep the young person informed of what is going on.

The plan is made to ensure the young person is kept safe and well and that they get any help they need. The plan will also show any other action that may be necessary.

What is a child protection register?

It is a list of children or young people who are considered to be suffering from or who are likely to suffer, significant harm. The reasons for a young person's name appearing on the register should be fully explained to them.

Why is there a list?

- To provide a list of children or young people in the area whom it is thought may be, or who are definitely, at risk.
- To provide a central point of reference for professional staff who are worried about a young person and want to know quickly whether a child protection plan exists.
- To provide information for all the professionals concerned.

When can my name come off the list?

- If the plan made at the Child Protection Conference is successful and it is thought that a young person is no longer at risk.
- If the reasons that originally led to the registration no longer apply.
- If the young person has moved to another area and that area has accepted responsibility for the case.
- When the young person is 18 years old.
- When the young person has married.
- If the young person has died.

The first two categories for de-registration always require a conference to take place. All other categories may be agreed without the need for a meeting.

How often do these meetings take place?

They must be held at least every six months to review the situation, more often if necessary, until such time as everyone agrees they are no longer required.

For further information, see the local authority Child Protection Procedures.

Working with parents

The law says that contact between a child who is looked after and their family, and those connected with them must be encouraged. As far as possible carers should work in partnership with parents. Even if a care order is in force, contact must be encouraged unless the order says otherwise.

Research has shown that a very large number of young people who are looked after return home again, often quite soon (Bullock, 1993). Department of Health yearly statistics also confirm this. Keeping contact with families is therefore especially important. It is **crucial** to make good links with a young person's family within the first weeks of them being looked after. This can determine how often a young person will meet up with the family in the future.

The young person's social worker should draw up a plan, as soon as possible, including showing contact with families. If the young person does not have a social worker, then the plan should be discussed with the team manager. Some local authorities may have different practices and you should ensure the guidelines are followed.

Partnership with families is the most important part. But it can be difficult when one side of the partnership does not want to take into consideration what the child's wishes are.

Carer

...on the other hand many young people resent the fact that parents who have not bothered about them in the past should suddenly be involved in decision making about their lives.

Carer

When they tell **me** *it's a good idea to see my family, I tell them where to go!*

Young person

As with every good tale, there are two sides to the story. Quite often you, as the carer, may feel like the 'pig in the middle'.

Remember to:
- Listen to what both sides have to say.
- Talk to the young person regularly, about all sorts of things. A young person will probably come round to talking about their family at some time.
- Find out all the facts you can; it may be that you should read the young person's file.
- Sometimes a brother, sister, grandparent, relative or friend can act as a go-between.
- Take things slowly, one step at a time; don't rush.
- If you arrange a first meeting, arrange it on neutral ground.
- If either party refuses to make contact at first, don't give up, but be sensitive to the difficulties.
- There will probably be lots of hate or hurt – explain things as you see them to both sides.

Most young people really do want contact with parents even if they won't admit it. The following are just two quotes, one from a girl and the other from a boy:

> *...we should try hard to stick with our families.*

> *...at the end of the day everyone has to have contact with their family.*

Encouraging contact with families

There are practical things that you could do to encourage keeping contact with families:

- When the young person comes to your home, get them to bring their own duvet or other items from their bedroom if possible. It may help them feel more secure and it will remind them of their home and their families.

- The parents could be involved with holidays, or outings, or on committees.

- Suggest the parents come to the home – if the local authority (or court) agrees.

- Suggest the young person visits their parents home for a short while, gradually building up to an overnight stay, then a weekend visit – if the local authority (or court) agrees. This contact needs to form part of the young person's overall plan.

- Once good contact is established parents could be asked to come to the home to help out in a practical way such as cooking, organising a visit or demonstrating a particular skill they may have.

Keeping parents in touch with what is going on in the young person's life is a good way of keeping them informed. It is much easier for parents to work in partnership if they are kept informed. The young person may be in touch, or willing to see, other family members, such as grandparents or aunts and uncles. This should be encouraged (providing the court or local authorities agree). It is a good way to maintain family links and it may lead to contact with parents in the future.

Once you have got the contact going, you will have to help to keep it going. You will probably also have to explain to both parties:

- Just what 'working in partnership' means in practice.

- What the benefits are for both sides.

- That talking and discussing are better than arguing and shouting.

However, if it really won't work out, have a plan ready so you know how you will handle the situation from both sides.

There may be other important people in a young person's life and they may need help to keep in touch with those people.

Of course there will be set backs, these are only to be expected. Act as a mediator if you can, by:

- Encouraging the contact.

- Keeping the contact going.

- Helping the young person to remember family birthdays.

- Inviting families to special events.

- Encouraging telephone contact and letters.

- Encouraging the exchange of photographs.

- Being welcoming when families come.

- Telling parents that their travelling expenses may be paid by the social services department.

- Sharing information.

It is a good idea for you to keep a record of whenever contact is made between families and the young person.

Collecting mementos

Talking about their past is often a very painful experience for young people and many don't want to do it. Others will be extremely keen to learn as much as they can. All young people have a past, a present, and a future. Wait until the time is right to talk to the young person about where they have lived, who they have lived with, what memories they have and what more they would like to know. **Collecting mementos** is a way of filling in the jigsaw of a young person's life, both in the past and for the future.

They may bring with them mementos that are important to them, or they may, out of choice, bring nothing, hoping to wipe out bitter memories. On the other hand they may have nothing to bring. What is a treasure to one young person may be trash to another. Respecting personal possessions may be a hard lesson for some young people to learn, but one worth learning. Everyone will be different and all your skill will be needed in this area.

You could keep an envelope handy for them where you or they can pop in mementos or photos and keep them safe. It's also worth keeping a good filing system going of negatives and of photographs taken, as it can be disappointing for the young person when they decide they want to remember a particular event and the negatives can't be found!

It is important that young people leave their placement with positive memories. Some young people may wish to do some **life work** (sometimes known as **life story work**) so the next part gives some more details.

Life (story) work

Life work (sometimes known as **life story work**) is a way of giving young people a chance to learn about their past life and history. It should help them to understand some of the things that have happened. Often the information is put together safely into an album which may be called a **life book**.

 But I know all about me!

- You might think you do but often your memory, or what you have been told, is not correct.
- Will you remember when you are an adult?
- Who will be around to tell you?

Some information will be on social services files but things like photographs and keepsakes need to be put together whilst they can still be found. Sadly though, information sometimes just cannot be found.

 How long will it take to do?

That depends on whoever is doing life work with the young person – but it might be once a week for say an hour or two. It depends on whether they will be going out to take photographs, make visits or whether it is just a question of organising what is already there.

Some ideas for life work:
- drawing family trees
- tracing maps
- putting photographs into an album
- writing down memories after a chat
- visiting cemeteries to look at gravestones

It all depends on how much the young person wants to include or how much research they want to do.

 Must I do it?

Everyone has a right to privacy so, of course, the answer is 'No'. Often young people who have left care say they wish they had done it. When they are older they will know things about themselves which they will be able to share with their own family and friends.

Whose book is it?

It belongs to the young person but you may offer to keep it in a safe place as photographs and keepsakes cannot be replaced. But it really is up to the young person what they do with it and to whom they show it. It is also a good idea to add to it with photographs and mementos of the young person's time being looked after.

Complaints

Positive complaining

Making a complaint should be seen as a positive step. It means the young person has:

- Thought about the situation.
- Decided that something is not right.
- Is willing to do something about it.

Homes that encourage criticism and comment will be better places in which to live – there's always room for improvement everywhere. It is healthy for moans to be discussed openly and everyone's point of view heard. One children's home manager said: 'We've only had 10 complaints this month.' She was disappointed, as she saw complaints from young people as a way of improving the care and service provided and of making the home a better place for the young people to live.

There are two different types of complaints.

1. The really serious ones which must be handled formally – see your organisation's complaints procedure.
2. Those which can be handled within the home, such as moans, suggestions and problems – the ones the manager was referring to.

> **What may seem unimportant to you may be very serious to a young person.**

Harassment and discrimination

Complaints about **sexual** or **racial harassment** or racial discrimination are important. You may be able to help or you may have to take the matter further.

Complaints procedure

Everyone should know what the **complaints procedure** is and how they go about making a complaint. If the information is not available the young person should be told how to get hold of the procedure. Carers in children's homes and foster carers will have their own complaints procedure which may not be the same as the one for young people. You should keep the young person informed of what is going on and let them know the outcome of the complaint. If the complaint is of a serious nature then the correct formal procedure for your authority must be followed.

Many young people feel that it is not worth making a complaint either because they might be victimised or because the system is stacked against them:

- Reassure them on both counts.
- Help them work out what they want to say.
- Support them in what they are trying to do.

Of course, you may not feel able to help them for all sorts of reasons. You should then put them in touch with someone who can. These might be:

- senior members of staff
- Citizen's Advice Bureaux
- local councillors
- ombudsmen
- the courts – young people can ask for a judicial review
- the local authority complaints office

Some hints for handling a complaint:

- Listen attentively to the young person's complaint. Make sure you fully understand it, take notes.
- Show that you understand their feelings and thank them for raising the matter.
- State your own position non-defensively and without hostility.
- Find out if the young person has any suggestions for resolving the complaint.
- If appropriate, say what you will do to correct the situation.
- Always set a specific follow-up date.

> **Always give them a copy of your notes or a copy of the formal complaint.**

Discrimination

 What does discrimination mean?

The dictionary definition is: 'to treat differently because of prejudice'.

 What are the main types of discrimination?

Direct discrimination: Direct discrimination happens when you are treated worse than others or segregated from them, because of your race, colour, nationality, or ethnic or national origin, disability, sex or sexual orientation.

Indirect discrimination: This is more complicated. It happens when everyone seems to be treated in the same way, but, in practice, people from a certain group are put at a greater disadvantage. The law says that when a rule hits a particular group harder than others (intentionally or not) and there's no good reason for the rule – it is indirectly discriminatory.

Victimisation: If you are victimised because you have complained about racial discrimination, or because you have supported someone else's complaint, this, too, is unlawful discrimination.

Discrimination applies to:

- jobs
- training
- housing
- education
- services – from councils, banks, insurance companies, pubs, clubs, discos, restaurants, cinemas, travel agencies and so on

It is important to realise that some people are discriminated against in more than one of these ways, falling into more than one of the groups which suffer discrimination, for example, they may be black and disabled.

 ## Why do people discriminate?

Some people discriminate because they do not like a particular group or situation. Many people discriminate without realising it. Most young black people in this country have British Nationality and have the same rights as everyone else. White young people often don't understand this. There are comparatively few black people living in this country (about 8% of the population at present), so when white young people, from mainly white areas, meet black people for the first time it can come as quite a culture shock.

Discrimination doesn't just mean treating someone differently; it also includes using names, or words, no matter how innocently, which put people down. If you hear name calling going on, ensure you discuss it. All too often young people don't realise how hurtful and cruel they are being.

Am I black or am I white?

> 'Am I black or am I white?
> I used to ask that question
> every day and night
> why do you ask a question
> as obvious as that?
> It's plain to see that you are black
> But being in care
> In a white community
> It's hard to decide
> with no black family'

Anon

These are the first two verses of a poem that highlight the problems of a black young person being cared for by white carers.

What does the law say?

The law says that due consideration should be made to the young person's religious persuasion, racial origin, cultural and linguistic background. Where young people are disabled the local authority must provide services to help the disabled to lead the lives they wish. What this means is recognising, respecting and meeting differences, supporting and building pride and esteem.

Recognising differences

Differences should not be ignored. People are not all the same. Some people have different skin colour, hair, religious backgrounds. They may practise different rites in relation to their culture. Some young people have different languages. Some young people may be in a wheelchair or have a speech impediment.

Respecting differences

No one should be discriminated against because of their difference. Young people may need your help to learn to respect differences.

Meeting racial, disability, religious, cultural, dietary and cosmetic needs

Young people may previously have been living with their own (natural) families or have been looked after away from their families. As their carer, you will need to find out what the young person has been used to and what practices they would like to follow. The young person may have strong views on whether or not they want for example to eat Asian or Caribbean food; attend a Mosque or West Indian Church; wear their hair in a particular way; be treated differently because of their disability.

Young people may:

- Want to know where to buy certain foods or cream for their hair or skin.
- Need to buy braille paper or find out how to get access to different places if they are in a wheelchair.
- Need support and help to explore different possibilities for their life.
- Need help so they feel confident about asking for and getting help.

Giving support

Sometimes young people may suffer harassment. They need help and guidance in all sorts of ways, for example on how to complain and who to complain to.

Colour and language

The language we use to describe ourselves and others can be very important in establishing self confidence and identity. In the UK at present, the term 'Black' is often used to cover a wide group of people from different countries. However, some people do not like this collective term and prefer their individual nationality to be used, e.g. Chinese,

Asian. The term 'Black' has been used by some as a political term of unity. You may feel it appropriate to discuss this with the young person in your care. If you feel you need any more information about looking after young people from cultural backgrounds different from your own, you may find it helpful to refer to the book published by the National Children's Bureau, *Religion, Ethnicity, Sex Education – Exploring the Issues*, which highlights the importance of understanding different cultural norms, such as those regarding puberty, circumcision etc. There will be other books obtainable from your local library that may also help.

Building pride and esteem

All young people need positive images of themselves, their background and way of life.

 How carers can help

- Find out all you can about the background, history and culture of any young person who lives with you. It may be something you could do together. Local libraries are a good starting point for this research; so is talking to the young person.

- Discuss with the young person what food they like to eat and then explore together the shops that sell such foods.

- Organise a meeting with other members of staff or young people to exchange information and ideas.

- Find out the names and addresses of local groups where young people can meet other people of their own culture or religion or other disabled young people if they wish.

If a young person feels they are being discriminated against you could help them make a complaint. They could contact any of the following:

- Citizens Advice Bureaux, or local advice and information centres.
- Commission for Racial Equality.
- Area office of social services department.
- Equal Opportunities Commission.
- Some local councils have set up offices (sometimes called Equal Opportunity Units) to deal with discrimination in housing, employment etc.
- Schools and colleges.
- Local authority complaints officer.
- Local church, gurudaware, mosque, Hindu temple – these will have people who are keen to speak to young people. Some have liaison workers.
- Youth centres or youth counselling services.
- Personnel manager, the person responsible for staff or the trade union representative if the young person is at work.

Disability and language

Advice and suggestions on terms to use and avoid when working with young people with disabilities, and also for helping young people who may have someone disabled living in the same home, are listed below.

- Do offer help, but don't get upset if it is rejected – sometimes it will be welcome, but sometimes it won't be needed or may hinder the disabled person from doing it in their own, possibly slower but effective way.

- Young people may become angry or aggressive as they try to come to terms with their disability or want to learn to become independent.

- Do not make assumptions.

- Don't make comments like 'I don't know how you manage' or 'I'd die if I was blind/deaf/couldn't walk'.

- Speak directly to the person, not to whoever may be with them. People still say 'Does he take sugar?'

- Obtain as much knowledge regarding the young person's special needs or disability as soon as possible.

- Have high but realistic expectations.

- Stress the good things.

- Praise, reassure.

- Encourage the young person to take part in a wide variety of activities.

- Help or teach them to play, find activities they can do individually, with groups in similar situations and with all young people.

- Help the young person to mix with others.

- Don't treat them differently but as individuals.

- Talk to them, discuss, explain.

- Sometimes young people with disabilities need firm boundaries. Set them.

- Be patient.

Introduction: where will I live?

Before a young person is looked after there should have been a planning meeting and all the necessary arrangements made. The aim, in most, but not all, cases will be to get a young person back living with their parents or guardians as soon as possible.

Wherever they live young people need to know what to expect and what the rules of the house are. Honestly tell them what the present situation is, such as how long they will be staying, whether they will be fostered short term or long term, etc. Many young people will definitely want to be fostered or definitely will not, preferring to live in a children's home. Their social worker should tell them about the options.

With the help of their social worker, if they have one, encourage the young person to visit the local children's homes, foster carers, or other future placements; to speak to the young people there and the carers: the young person will then be better able to make informed choices about where they would like to live.

foster homes

 Being fostered, what does it mean?

It means a young person (and hopefully any brothers and sisters) will be **looked after** by another person, called a **foster carer** in the foster carer's own home. This may be either for a short time while things are sorted out at home or for a longer period, depending on the situation.

 Can anyone be a foster carer?

No, anyone can apply but they are carefully chosen.

 What happens?

Once the young person has decided they would like to be fostered, social services will try to find a foster carer who is suitable. Someone who:

- Has the same background and racial origin.
- Has the same religion (if they have one).
- Understands their needs.
- Lives close by so they can attend the same school.
- Has other children in their family or does not have any children depending on the young person's needs.

The young person should visit the carer's house, perhaps several times. The young person and the carer then decide whether they think they will be suitable for each other. Once this is agreed social services will make all the necessary arrangements. Their social worker or key worker should call regularly.

The foster family will do what they think is best and will treat the young person as part of their family. If the foster family is from a different racial background, the social worker or whoever is responsible will try to ensure the young person has contact with people of similar background.

Although every care is taken to make a young person's stay with a foster family successful, sometimes it just does not work out. This may be through no fault of anyone; circumstances may change or a young person who thought they would like to be fostered finds out that it is not for them.

Children's homes

 ## What are they?

Children's homes are houses of varying sizes that provide young people who cannot live at home with the best possible quality of life in the circumstances. They are run by social services or organisations such as Barnardo's or Catholic Children's Homes with a team of staff, usually led by a manager, who will be on duty on a rota basis 24 hours a day, 365 days a year.

Sometimes the home will be separated into sections so that part of it will be made into small flats, often called **independent units**, where young people can learn skills such as budgeting and cooking, to help them prepare for when they are no longer 'looked after'. Sometimes their stay will be short lived and they can go back to living with their parents.

A keyworker is normally allocated to each young person who should also have a social worker. If this is not the case then the keyworker may be asked to undertake some social work duties such as acting as advocate for the young person on a temporary basis.

The young person will be encouraged to attend school, college or work regularly, to bring friends to the home and to act responsibly around the house: the house rules are often set in partnership with the young people.

Secure children's homes

 ## What are they?

Secure children's homes are buildings specially designed for young people whose liberty needs to be restricted. Some secure accommodation will be attached to a children's home: others will be located separately. It may be necessary for a young person to be housed in secure accommodation outside their area if there are no facilities or vacancies locally. No one under the age of 13 years may be placed in secure accommodation without the permission of the Secretary of State, nor can they be kept in a secure children's home for more than 72 hours over any one period of 28 days without a court order.

When might I be sent to a secure children's home?

There are very severe regulations on when a young person's liberty can be restricted. If the young person has **not** committed an offence a young person should only be placed in secure accommodation if:

- The young person has a history of absconding and is likely to abscond from any other type of accommodation; and if, when the young person absconds, they are likely to suffer significant harm.

- The young person is kept in any other type of accommodation they are likely to injure themselves or other people.

The court has the power to send young offenders to secure accommodation in certain circumstances. A young person placed in secure accommodation will have all normal rights except freedom to leave the building.

The home environment

The best children's home I ever visited had been the family house of the home manager and her husband and which had been converted to a children's home. It felt like a home, it looked like home. It was home to all the residents, both long term and short term stayers, and as such was respected by them.

The environment in which we all live is really important, much more important than many realise. A young person said that although the staff seemed nicer at a particular home she wouldn't go there because 'It was a mess – how could I take my friends to a place like that?'

It is important to involve young people in how the home is organised and decorated as this will help them establish an identity, a sense of belonging.

What can I do around the house?

Involve young people in:

- Choosing colour schemes.
- Where possible in actually decorating, not just their room but other parts of the house.
- Choosing any new furniture, equipment or pictures.
- Changing the layout of different parts of the house.
- Taking responsibility for the care and cleaning of the house or their room.

What can I do in my room?

Young people should have their own room: if that's not possible, their own space in an agreed part of a room where they can put up pictures, posters etc.

- Let them be responsible for keeping it clean and tidy.
- If they are sharing, let them agree the ground rules with the other occupant.
- Give them a key to their room; only go in their room when they are not there if it is essential.
- Young disabled people should be helped to live a full life; you may have to make changes around the home.

> **Things that may seem unimportant at the time may have more of an impact than you think.**

If something gets broken or damaged, don't just leave it or call in the expert to do the job. If possible, work with the young person who caused the damage or any others interested in putting it right. They'll respect it more next time.

A few indoor plants here and there will give a good feeling to a home – possibly grown by the young people, and certainly nurtured by them. Let them cut the grass or hoe the flower beds. Not only will they be learning life skills but will get the satisfaction from a job well done and be able to admire the results of their efforts.

If food is set out with care it seems to taste much better. If you set standards many young people will learn what is possible and remember it for the future

Everyone, whether male or female, should try to make that little extra effort with the way they look. Set an example. The young people will notice. They may laugh at you or compliment you but they will notice. You'll set a standard for them to follow. It is all part of building up their confidence, making them feel important and making them feel they are taking part in decisions, no matter how small an effect it has on their lives.

Introduction: money matters!

The way allowances work does not help the young people to get a sense of reality

Carer

If you don't ask, you don't get it.

Young person

It ought to be written down the money you're entitled to.

Young person

I share with the young people how much money we have. I think the reality that there is only so much money available is useful for them to know.

Children's home manager

Young people and carers agree that:

- Learning to manage money is an important skill.
- Knowing what is available and how it is shared out is important – it gives them a sense of reality.
- Young people should be told what everyone is entitled to and why. It will help them understand why some young people seem to get more than others.
- Young people need to know so they can make choices in their day-to-day lives.
- Young people should be involved in decision making on how the money is spent so they can learn to plan for their future.

 What are you entitled to?

Some local authorities give clear guidelines on how money should be allocated and spent. Others leave it to the discretion of foster carers, home managers, social workers and even area managers. Whatever the system, young people need to be told about it; to be told what they will get both now and in the future; and they need to be involved in deciding how any special allowances are spent. They may also need your help to get it!

True story: it's your money

A young man from Birmingham was very upset because his carer had decided, without consultation with him, that a particular allowance should be spent on a personal stereo and tapes of his native language, Punjabi. He desperately wanted a pair of special trainers similar to those worn by the rest of his basketball team. He gave up playing in the team because he was too embarrassed to wear his own trainers. He flatly refused to listen to the tapes. He was very angry and resentful. The carer, with the best will in the world, was giving 'due consideration to the child's religious persuasion, racial origin, cultural and linguistic background' but not considering the rights and responsibilities of that young person as an individual.

This is a difficult area as someone may always feel unjustly treated, but if money matters are discussed freely, then young people will know what to expect and when. Special circumstances for giving extra money should be kept to a minimum:

> *I would give the girls about ten pounds each month and call it health money so they can buy their own toiletries etc.*

Carer

Local authorities are required to provide money for young people who wish to further their education and for those young people 'leaving care':

- Find out exactly what money is available.

- Work hard to make sure they get it.

- Make sure young people are treated fairly.

- Make sure young people know well in advance what they can expect.

They'll thank you for it! Money matters must be seen to be fair.

Any young person who is employed should be expected to contribute towards their maintenance, pay for their own clothing and their personal expenses. If their wages are insufficient to meet all these costs, the local authority should ensure that the foster carer is not receiving less maintenance, nor the young person less than their peers. This also applies to young people who are in full time education who may receive additional allowances. The following is a simple suggested formula to work out a weekly contribution if a young person gets a job:

- Agree with the young person what the take home pay is – excluding overtime payments or bonuses etc.

- Deduct weekly fares and lunch allowance.

- One quarter of the remainder is what the young person should contribute to their upkeep.

> *They need to be encouraged to save because when they leave care the money will have to cover bills, rent, food, as well as having a good time.*

Carer

Managing money

> *My friends think I'm better off being 'in care'.*

Young person

...and, of course, they may be right from a material point of view. It would seem to an outsider that there is an allowance for everything – a new bike, for outings, school trips, for hobbies and clothes. Learning how to manage money is important to everyone.

Young people who are living in a children's home or a foster home will need special help in this area, as their circumstances may never be quite the same again.

Keeping a **budget plan** is a good idea to help them manage their money. On page 37 is one they might like to use.

 Money – what do I need to think about?

- What they need each week.
- Where the money will come from.
- Whether it will cover their expenses.
- If it won't, what they can do about it.

Young people also need to learn about the reasons and importance of saving money and the different methods available to them.

Bank accounts and savings

Many young people (and adults too) like to have cash, because it is easier to use. However, it is also easier to spend, which may often mean wasting money. Cash can also get stolen or lost. It is a good idea to encourage the young person to open a bank or building society account and to only draw out so much money at a time.

Banks and building societies are keen to give advice and help. Research shows that once a person joins a particular organisation they very often stay with that bank or building society throughout their life. These companies offer a variety of inducements to get a young person to join and it may be you could work out together which one offers the best value for money. Offers may include record vouchers, train tickets, free overdraft (not to be recommended), additional interest or no bank charges.

To open an account a young person will need:
- Some form of identification such as passport, ID card or driving licence.
- Letter of introduction from an adult.
- Letter of introduction from a school or college.
- A small amount of money.

They will also need to go along to meet someone from the bank or building society. Before this they should have obtained, and gone through, the leaflets from the different banks to see which one suits them best.

Avoiding debt

Even the cleverest person sometimes gets in a muddle with money, so it's important that young people understand how difficult budgeting is, and that they get plenty of practice before becoming independent. Everyone's needs are different, and so is what is important to them. Here are a few ideas on how you could help young people to save on outgoings: the list is based on one produced by the Fostering Network.

 ## How can I cut down on my expenses?

- Buy clothes that last and won't go out of fashion too quickly.
- Buy clothes at sale time.
- Don't buy clothes which are 'dry clean only' – they are expensive to clean.
- Washing clothes by hand is cheaper than the launderette or washing machine.
- Walk, if possible, rather than use bus, car or train – it's healthier and saves money.
- Use a bike – buy a second-hand one through adverts in newspapers, or go to auctions.
- Use the library for books, CDs, cassettes and videos.
- Avoid late-night corner shops, because, although they tend to be convenient, they are expensive.
- Buy groceries etc. in bulk with friends. If they're becoming independent soon, perhaps it's something a group could do together.
- Cook for friends – take it in turns – it's often cheaper and gives more variety.
- Get a season ticket if you travel regularly.
- Car boot sales, jumble sales, markets and auctions can provide good cheap finds, whether it's clothing, furniture, books or other household goods.
- Get a free haircut by being a model on a training night at the local hairdressers' training school.
- Keep heating bills down by making sure there are draft excluders around doors and windows.
- Wear more clothes, rather than turning up the heating.
- Ready-cooked and take-away food can be expensive, so try cooking more meals from scratch; fresh vegetables are cheap to buy and very nourishing.
- Buying meat from a local butcher is often cheaper than supermarkets and they usually sell cheaper cuts as well.
- Avoid buying goods on credit or hire purchase (also known as HP) – it's expensive and can get out of control.
- Giving up or reducing smoking is not just good for health but it is an excellent way of saving money!

 ## What about debt?

Should a young person get into debt, they will also need to know where they can go for help and advice. Is there a debt counsellor in your area? Is there someone from social services who could help?

Managing money, budgeting, savings CHECKLIST

Fill in these charts to work out where your money is going.

Outgoings	Weekly	Monthly	Annually
Rent			
Food			
Travel			
Clothes			
TV Licence and/or rental			
Council tax			
Water rates			
Electricity			
Gas			
Laundry			
Cleaning materials			
Soap, make-up, deodorant etc.			
Drink			
Cigarettes			
Presents			
Entertainment			
Credit/HP/loans			
Other			
Total			

Income	Weekly	Monthly	Annually
Take-home pay			
Benefits			
Housing benefits			
Other			
Total			

Income			
Outgoings			
What's left?			

Notes

Education and spare time

Education is the key to a successful future.

Government minister

Problems and solutions

Education is a good way to build a sound future. Lots of recent research about young people has shown how worried they are about their education. Young people really need your help to get the best from education.

Possible **problems**:

- Young people get worried that they are getting behind with their work because of poor attendance; this often makes them not want to go to school which makes matters worse.

- Perhaps their concentration has not been as good as it should be – worries, disturbances or neglect may well be the cause.

- Young people may have had frequent changes of schools.

- The time taken to get a young person into a school after a move was too long.

- A young person may not have been getting enough extra help to enable them to catch up.

- Home tutoring has not been available soon or often enough if there was a problem with school.

- Quite often there has been no place that was quiet where they could do their homework.

- Sometimes young people may have been treated differently at school.

- If they are disabled they might have problems moving about the building.

- A young person may have been teased.

- A young person may lack confidence to ask the teacher if they don't understand.

- A young person may not have any friends at the school, so misbehaves or 'shows off' to draw attention to themselves.

- A young person may need help to build up their self-esteem and confidence (see page 72).

These and other problems will need your help. Here are some **solutions** other carers have suggested:

- Make a nuisance of yourself with the education office to get things speeded up, in order to get a young person back into school, or being home tutored, or anything else that may be needed.

- Help them with their weaker subjects, such as reading or spelling, possibly without the other young people knowing, so they don't lose face.

- If you don't feel you can help them with their homework or schoolwork, find someone else who can help them.

- Local authorities should have a person who has responsibility for the young person's education. Contact them and ask for their advice or help.

- If the young person is disabled make sure the school has suitable access facilities. You may also have to help to get them into the school building.

- Make sure there is a place set aside especially for homework.

- Attend open evenings, school events and sports days.

- Work with all concerned to ensure they have an education plan, and that it is up-to-date and relevant, and then help the young person to achieve their targets.

- Have high but realistic expectations.

- Encourage them, praise them, and show an interest in all they do.

- Show you care.

A very few young people will find that the education system does not meet their needs. Work-based alternatives may be the answer. The social services person responsible for education will advise you. The question of feeling that they are being treated differently because of where they are living is not a new one. It may be due to a lack of understanding or genuine concern but, if it is upsetting the young person, then you may need to go to the school to try to sort out the problem.

Many examinations include a good deal of coursework, so if a young person changes school at 14, 15 or 16 years, they may not be able to take all their exams. It is especially important that 'all the stops are pulled out' to try to get the young person to stay at the same school if possible. There may also be other ways of getting round problems of changing school and missing class work. Ask the education office. On the next few pages are some questions that could apply to any young person. Take the time to go over the points with them, and the changes in their school life will be much smoother and less of a worry. For young people not to be educated to their full potential is not acceptable. If neither you nor the young person's social worker get anywhere, you could try contacting:

- your local councillor

- the social services person responsible for liaison with education

- the education office

- in fact anyone you think might help

Education: a young person's questions

Moving to another home doesn't necessarily mean you have to change schools, but sometimes you will have to choose another school to go to. Most people change schools around their 11th birthday anyway.

If I have to change schools how do I choose a new one?

There may not be much choice, depending on where you live, but if you have to choose a new school, your carer can go with you to look round a few schools. Talk to the teachers and pupils and then decide, providing there is a vacancy.

What will it be like starting a new school?

Some things may be done differently. Just remember:
- That everyone takes time to settle in somewhere new.
- To ask if you're not sure about anything.
- To talk any problems over with your carer or your friends.

How do I choose which subjects to study?

When a young person is 13 or 14, they will have to decide which subjects they want to study until they are 16. You will be given talks on the subjects you can do, and will probably have handouts to read.

Ask the teachers, and yourself:
- How interesting do you find the subjects?
- Will they help you get the job you want?
- Will there be a lot of reading to do?
- Will there be a lot of practical things to do?

The young person won't have a completely free choice because:
- The law says you **must** learn certain subjects, such as maths and English.
- Some subjects may clash on the school timetable.

What can I do when I'm 16?

At 16, young people can:
- Go on to get more qualifications.
- Start a skills course at college, such as bricklaying, gardening or word processing.
- Find a job.
- Start on a training scheme.
- Improve their maths and English.

Why should I stay on at school or college?

- Many jobs need trained workers.
- Pay and prospects are likely to be better after further study.
- You will have a wider choice of jobs or careers.

What qualifications will I need?

For some courses you will need to get certain grades in your examinations. For others, you will only have to show you want to work hard.

What if I fail some of my exams?

You can re-take most exams you fail – many people spend an extra year doing this – but it might be better for you to do a vocational (job-related) course instead. Your school, college or personal adviser will help you decide.

How long do courses last?

Most courses last one or two years. Young people can apply to any college or school they wish but help with transport expenses will only be given in certain cases. Visit several different places where you could go with your carer, and find the one that suits you best.

What will it be like?

There will be a lot of work to do, and much of it will have to be done in your own time. You will also have to learn to attend on time and regularly without constant reminders. It will be hard work and you should expect this, but you will also find you are treated more like an adult than when you were at school. At college there will be all sorts of different people of all ages over 16. It will take a lot of getting used to. Stick at it and get the qualifications you really deserve.

What if I have disabilities or special needs?

Young people who have disabilities may take examinations that have been adapted to meet a particular disability e.g. Braille question paper, or be given extra time in which to complete the examination paper. Most schools or colleges will nominate a particular teacher, for example, a year tutor, who will be responsible for you. They will have a supportive and liaising role. They will be the person to contact if there is a problem. This teacher will be responsible for your emotional and social development as well as your educational development.

If you have been out of school for some time it may be possible for the school to allow you phased re-introduction into school life – that means coming in for part of a day or week until you feel settled.

Teachers are really pleased when carers come into school to see them. They want carers to work with teachers to improve the education of all young people.

Qualifications

Choices, choices, choices. It does seem that the more qualifications you have, the more choices you will have in getting a job, choosing a job you like, moving to another job and getting promotion. There are so many qualifications available at present that many people are not sure what they mean and how the levels compare with one another. The Qualifications and Curriculum Authority (QCA) in England has been working with officers in Wales and Northern Ireland to produce a national framework of qualifications. They have also been working with the Scottish Authorities to ensure the vocational qualifications already in place remain aligned to each other.

In the future, the aim is to ensure that the assessment of all qualifications will meet the same rigorous high quality of standards across the UK. Your school, college, careers service, Connexions adviser or social services education person should be able to give you details of the different qualifications and what they mean. You can also look on the web under QCA to get the most up-to-date information.

Part-time jobs

 Can I have a part-time job?

Yes, when you are 13. But you **must** have a work permit until you are 16. Some local authorities may do things differently, but the principle is the same.

 Why must I have a work permit?

To make sure that:

- You are covered by insurance if you have an accident.
- The employer obeys the law.

 How do I get a work permit?

A young person can get a form from their new employer, from their school, or from the education office.

What do I do with the form?

Make sure that every part of the form is filled in, and that the employer sends it to the address shown on the form before you start work. You will be sent an employment card which you must keep in case an inspector asks to see it.

What sort of work can and can't I do?

- Young people can't start work before 7 o'clock in the morning, or work after 7 o'clock in the evening.

- On school days they can't work for more than two hours a day. They can only work for one hour before school starts.

- No person under 16 or who is of compulsory school age can work:
    - in a quarry or a mine
    - in a factory
    - in the transport industry
    - collecting or sorting refuse
    - in a fish shop
    - in delivering milk
    - on a building site
    - in telephone sales/canvassing making house-to-house collections

- Young people can't serve alcohol or petrol until they are 18.

See www.careersdirect.org.uk for further information.

Leisure: what to do in your free time

Nothing succeeds like success.

B. Kahan

Young people will find life more fun if they have interests outside the home. It will:

- Help them build self-confidence.
- Give them a purpose, something to aim for, to achieve.
- Help them make new friends.
- Give them somewhere different to go. This is especially important when they 'leave care'.

Many young people will need a lot of help and encouragement to begin with.

I like sport, what can I do?

Many towns have swimming pools, skating rinks, sports and leisure centres, tennis courts, five-a-side football pitches etc. The young person could use any of these, or join a team and play football, basketball, netball, volleyball etc. There are sports that disabled young people can take part in, such as wheelchair basketball, hockey or tennis. Many areas offer cheaper prices for young people.

I like music, what can I do?

They could:

- Learn to play a musical instrument.
- Form or join a band.
- Make a tape.
- Go to gigs or concerts.

I like 'arty' things, what can I do?

They could:

- Paint, draw, act, make music, or just listen or watch.
- Join clubs for photography, stamp collecting etc.
- Go to art galleries or museums.
- Look for leaflets in their local library about classes, exhibitions or clubs, or go to their local arts centre and talk to the people there.

Can I join a club?

There are a variety of youth clubs offering many different activities for young people. There are also uniformed groups, such as guides and scouts. They are a good way of making new friends and none of them cost very much to join or to attend.

The local youth service may be helpful in putting black young people in touch with others, and in helping disabled young people to take part in their chosen activities by advising them on access to the various clubs etc. Many young people will feel too shy to join a club. Why not ask a friend to go with them? Tell them it can be fun when they start something new – and it will give them something to talk about with their friends, or with adults, or at job or college interview.

What else is there to do?

- Young people may like to attend a church, mosque, synagogue. They will meet many new people and make new friends.

- There are countryside and environmental projects to take part in or visit.

- It is worth visiting village halls, community schools and community centres to find out what is going on there.

- Go rock climbing, scrambling, abseiling; mountain bike riding; go on adventure holidays.

- If you don't want to go to a club or take part in sport, there are plenty of other things to do, such as reading, making your own clothes, cooking or woodworking. Try learning a new skill.

- Consider becoming a volunteer, in anything from helping old people to protecting the environment. Think of something that really interests you, and then find out how you can go about helping.

To find out more, there will be leaflets at:

- local library

- local arts centre

- sports or leisure centre

- education office

- youth and community service offices

- National Youth Agency

Doing something in your spare time can help when you apply for a job. For example, if you were a member of a netball team or football team it could show that you:

- Are reliable – turning up for each match.

- Are punctual.

- Can follow the rules.

- Get on well with others.

- Can work as part of a team.

- Have leadership qualities.

- Have self-discipline.

- Can make a regular commitment.

Do you know where the information on leisure activities is kept in your home? Is there a file for everyone to use?

I don't want to do anything!

It requires considerable confidence to try something new. Remember those fears 'Will I make a fool of myself'? Some young people may have had their self-esteem so battered by their experiences that they may want to stay in bed all day or mope around. A carer's motivational skills may be sorely tried, before a young person takes up a new interest. An invitation to come and see, rather than come and sign up, is often the best approach.

The electronic age: TV, computer games and surfing the net

There is a great deal of debate at present about the pros and cons of young people watching TV, playing computer games and using the Internet. There is, however, very little absolutely concrete evidence on either side. What is known is:

- If a young person has a tendency to have epileptic fits, then TV or computer screens may start them off because of what is known as 'flicker fusion'.

- If you ask young people from 6-16 years, they will tell you that some computer games make them feel frustrated and even violent.

- It would seem that watching violence on TV may also give a young person violent feelings or desires to experiment.

- Watching TV, playing computer games or surfing the net means a young person is inactive, not talking to other people, getting fresh air, playing with others, or getting exercise.

- A young person may have difficulty discerning fact from fiction.

- Some TV programmes billed as for young people are totally unsuitable in their use of language and presentation.

Computer games can help a young person with their school work, and certainly will help their hand-eye co-ordination, and can give many young people a great deal of pleasure. Watching TV can also be pleasurable; it can teach young people about current affairs, wildlife and nature and many other interesting topics. It can also fill a need for lonely young people as they feel the presenters are their friends.

A true story

Aysha was a Muslim aged 15. She had two sisters, one slightly older and one a little younger. They were all bought up in a very traditional fashion. Her teacher was amazed when she overheard Aysha talking about the most explicit sordid and sexual events. It transpired that she and her sisters hired pornographic videos from the local shop, taking them home in different covers and watching them in their room – a case of no-one checking on what the young people were watching.

What carers can do

- Discuss very carefully the TV programmes and video games the young person should watch or play and help the young person to learn to choose selectively.

- Monitor the use of the Internet.

- Never leave a young person alone watching TV for long periods.

- Sit with them; discuss what has happened and what you both have seen, think and feel about what you have seen.

- Agree on the amount of time in a day a young person may sit in front of a screen.

- Plan other activities to replace screen watching.

- Encourage the young person to take part in other activities as suggested above.

- Censor the videos, computer games or Internet a young person has access to. Some people are not always careful and leave unsuitable material lying around or available.

- Show an interest in the computer games; use them with the young person; talk about them. In this way unsuitable material should not be brought into your home.

- Be aware that the young person may be under pressure from their peers to play particular computer games or watch particular TV programmes.

- Talk with parents about which TV programmes the young person watches if this is appropriate.

It has also been discovered that in addition to young people being addicted to computer games, there is now an accepted psychological disorder called IAD (Internet Addiction Disorder) for people who cannot stop surfing the net. Some internet providers provide control systems as part of their monthly packages. It is also possible to buy programmes which cut out upsetting or inappropriate activities. Many young people access internet chat rooms. This is fraught with dangers. Paedophiles are known to pose as a young person in order to make contact with young people both of the same sex and the opposite sex.

Never let a young person meet someone from a chat line unaccompanied.

Never let them give out any personal information over the net.

Always warn, and remind them, of the dangers.

Section 6
Health

Introduction: taking action

Good health is important to everyone. Gradually, young people must learn to take responsibility for their own health.

 ## Why is good health important?

Good health is important because young people:

- If they are ill or have an accident will get better more quickly.
- WIll probably get ill less often anyway.
- WIll be better able to cope with stress.
- WIll probably do better at school – an old saying is 'a sound mind in a sound body'.
- WIll have less time off school, or work, so will make better progress.

Staying healthy

 ## What can we do to stay healthy?

1. Exercise
Everyone needs **exercise** because it will help stamina, strength and overall fitness. It will help their heart and lungs to work better, stop flabby muscles, keep weight down and generally help them cope with life better.

2. Sleep
No two people need exactly the same amount of sleep but **regular sleep is essential**. Get young people to work out what's best for them.

3. Diet
This doesn't just mean losing weight. It means thinking about what they eat, how much they eat and why they need certain foods.

Some foods that are good are:

- fresh fruit and vegetables
- pasta
- wholemeal bread
- low fat milk
- unsaturated margarine
- white meat
- fish

Some foods that are not very good are:

- crisps
- chocolate
- sweets
- cakes
- fizzy drinks

It's not as bad as it sounds! Together you can experiment with different recipes. The 'not so good' foods are not of course forbidden, but it **is** a good idea:

- To cut down on the amount of these a young person eats and drinks.
- To grill food instead of frying it.
- To reduce the amount of sugar and salt a young person eats.

If a young person is, or wishes to become, a vegetarian, care has to be taken to ensure a balanced diet. The Vegetarian Society or your GP will give details.

4. Weight

Find out what a young person's ideal weight is and try to get them to stay somewhere near that – sometimes easier said than done! A doctor or nurse will tell them what their weight should be, and weighing machines in chemists shops usually have a chart.

5. Smoking

Smoking kills. Smoking causes cancer.

These are just two statements that must now be printed on cigarette packets as a warning. The biggest single thing anyone can do to prevent heart disease is to not smoke, or to give up smoking.

There is a lot of pressure for young people to smoke – from their peers, from films and TV and from older people they admire. It is illegal for young people under 16 to buy cigarettes or tobacco. Education about the dangers of smoking is a must for everyone. Too often smoking is seen as a normal part of growing up without anyone realising the harm it causes. It is addictive, so giving up will not be easy. It is also expensive.

Reducing or **giving up smoking** should be encouraged. Don't preach, just **encourage** – the decision must be their own. You could agree a programme to give up smoking with them and help them stick to it.

Passive smoking is breathing other people's cigarette smoke. Until recently most people were unaware of the dangers. Not only can it cause irritation to eyes, nose and throat, headaches, dizziness and sickness; it can cause asthma and allergies to worsen and increase the risk of cancer by up to 30 per cent.

In reality many young people who are looked after are smokers. They are often physically and emotionally dependent on cigarettes so it may be necessary to work with the young people to set permissible boundaries that are acceptable to smokers and non-smokers alike. There are many programmes of support for people wanting to stop smoking – your GP surgery should be able to advise. Also, it may be possible for young people over the age of 16 years to obtain nicotine replacement treatment (NRT) from their GP to help them kick the habit.

House rules on smoking must be kept by everyone.

---

6. Alcohol

Like tobacco, alcohol is a drug. As with all drugs, if it is not used sensibly it can cause problems. Drinking too much alcohol can damage health.

Try to persuade young people not to drink heavily just because other people do. It won't make them look big; they will look just the opposite if they have too much – and they'll feel terrible the next day. They may also do things they and you wish they hadn't when they've been drinking alcohol, but this could be another topic for discussion.

The following drinks each contain 1 unit of alcohol:

- 1 single pub measure of spirits
- 1 single glass of sherry or fortified wine
- 1 small glass of table wine
- ½ pint of ordinary lager, beer or cider
- ¼ pint of strong lager, beer or cider

Bacardi Breezers contain 1½ units and spirit mixers even more.

As a rough guide, a man should not drink more than 21 units a week, and a woman no more than 14 units a week. **Young people should drink much less than this because alcohol is more likely to be harmful while they are still growing.**

If a young person does come home drunk:

- Try to keep them quiet so they don't disturb the rest of the house (easier said than done!). They may also be embarrassed the next morning so would prefer as few people as possible to know.
- If they want to talk, listen.
- If they want a drink, give them water or a cup of tea; sit with them.
- If they want to lay down, take them to their room. Wait until they are in bed. Turn them on their side so they don't inhale any vomit. Give them a bowl to be sick into. Before you leave them, let them know they can call you at any time.

7. Personal hygiene

Make sure young people know about the need to wash thoroughly, and use a deodorant at least once a day. They should also wash their hands after using the toilet.

Changing into clean clothes regularly is essential. Young people also need to be told of the consequences if they don't! With the changes that take place in both boys and girls during puberty it is particularly important that personal hygiene is stressed.

8. Sun

Too many young people think having a suntan not only makes them feel good but they think it gives them sex appeal too! It has now been proved that spending too much time in the sun is not a good idea and can cause skin cancer. Here are a few tips:

- **Above all, don't burn,** tan slowly – gradually increasing the time spent in the sun each day.
- Always use the appropriate sunscreens for different types of skin.
- Avoid the midday sun.
- Wear a sun hat.
- Wear a good pair of sunglasses.

Everyone's skin can burn but people with fair skin, usually those with blond or red hair, are particularly vulnerable.

9. Noise

Having very loud music in their ears from a personal stereo really can damage their hearing, and so can loud music in a disco or club. This hearing loss cannot be put right later.

10. Preventative medicine

Preventative medicine empowers everyone to take control of their lives. It can range from self-examination of breasts and testicles to awareness of the possible side-effects of prescribed drugs. The diet and lifestyle of young people can have a significant effect on their health in later life.

Other areas that are important are:

- Trying to reduce accidents amongst young people, especially those accidents which occur in the home.
- Persuading young people to wear protective clothing on motor bikes including properly fitting helmets - this applies equally to the rider and the passenger.
- Encouraging young people to take cycling proficiency tests and to wear cycle helmets.
- Reminding them that accidents are common whilst under the influence of drugs or alcohol.
- Encouraging them to give up smoking.

11. Advice and confidentiality

Sometimes young people find it easier to talk to outsiders about health matters. For free and confidential advice they can go to:

- their local doctor
- the school or college nurse
- a youth counsellor with responsibility for health
- family planning clinics

12. Medicals

If a young person is asked to have a medical they have the right to refuse, providing they are of a sufficient age to understand what is going on.

Other health issues

Periods

Many young girls will start their periods at 10 or 11 years of age, others will start much later. Whenever it is they need to be prepared, both physically and mentally. They need to know about:

- Sanitary towels and tampons – they should always have a packet stored in their bedroom so they are ready for the start of their periods.
- Period pains.
- Vaginal discharge that starts sometime before their periods begin.
- The many bodily changes that will be occurring at that time.

Help them to look forward to this new phase in their life.

There are many myths and different beliefs surrounding puberty both from a cultural and religious point of view. Local health promotion clinics or sexual health clinics should be able to provide information and advice. The Commission for Racial Equality also has specialists who may advise you if you need further information.

Eating disorders

This is the term used to describe irregular and potentially harmful eating habits and patterns. Two particular ones to be aware of are:

1. **Anorexia nervosa**, with sufferers described as anorexic (not eating).
2. **Bulimia nervosa** with sufferers known as bulimic (eating too much and then making themselves sick, or taking laxatives to clear out the bowels).

Many specialists believe the two disorders are part of the same illness. In fact, bulimics have often been anorexics first. Nine out of ten people showing signs of eating disorders are women, the peak age being between 15 and 18 years.

Eating disorders are often an indication of a person's feelings about themselves. They are emotional disorders which focus on food and consumption. People who suffer may have:

- A drive to become thin.

- An obsession with food, weight, calories etc.

- A reliance on eating or refusing to eat in order to cope with emotional discomfort, stress or developmental changes.

- A view that the world values appearances over personality.

Research has shown that young people who suffer from eating disorders:

- May have been 'easy' children who did not answer back

- Made less fuss and got less angry.

- Are often good students and high achievers.

- May be anxious to please and to live up to other people's expectations of them.

- Are often very secretive and try to hide their illness.

**Stress, anxiety, loneliness and depression may
trigger off anorexia or bulimia.**

If you think there is a problem, the young person should contact their GP or the Eating Disorders Association. They may need your help to do this.

Contraception

There are many different types of contraception. Advice on the best methods for them and on how to use the particular form of contraception is available from family planning clinics, GP surgeries, sexual health clinics and youth advisory centres. What is important is that young people are able to discuss contraception within a framework of relationships and responsibility (see Section 8).

See the diagram on the next page.

Condoms

Condoms are an effective form of birth control and will also help prevent the spread of disease from infected semen but care must be taken whenever a condom is used to ensure it is applied carefully and that it does not split. Young people need to understand that condoms are the most effective in preventing the spread of disease but may not be the most reliable in terms of preventing pregnancy, unless they are used with extreme care.

When having anal sex, a strong condom should always be used.

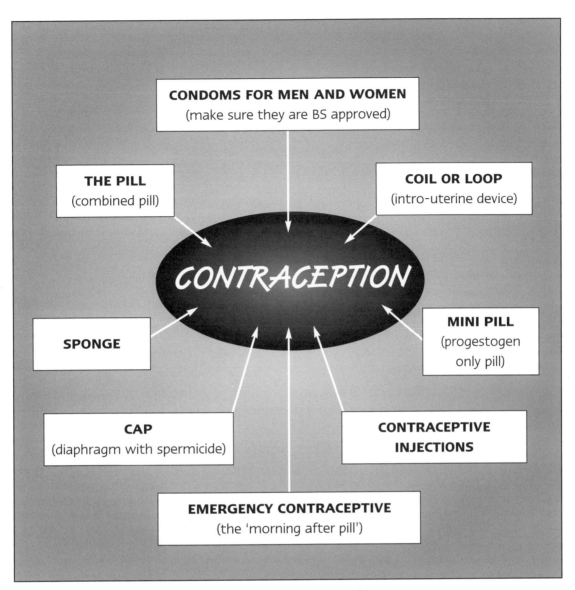

Figure 6: Contraception

The pill

The pill is also another reliable method of contraception but young people should be told about the possible side effects, both short- and long-term that may be caused by taking the pill.

HIV/AIDS

- **HIV** is a virus that can get into the blood and destroy the white blood cells leaving the body open to attack from other infections.
- **AIDS** is a condition which develops when the body's defences are not working properly. This means people are more likely to get illnesses which the body would normally be able to fight off easily.

These illnesses can be serious or fatal since, at the moment, there is no treatment which can cure AIDS.

How is the HIV virus passed on?

- Through intimate unprotected sexual contact, ie intercourse, between a man and a woman, between men or between women, if one of them has the virus.

- Needles or syringes which have been used by an infected person. Drug misusers are especially at risk.

- Occasionally women who have the virus can pass it on to their babies during pregnancy, at birth or through breast milk.

You cannot catch the virus by touching objects used by an infected person or by touching an infected person. All donated blood used in hospitals is now tested before it is used and blood products are heat-treated to reduce the risk of infection.

Young people will have heard a lot about HIV and AIDS and will often be scared because of what they have heard. Talk to them openly about sex and personal relationships (page 83) and about drug taking. If they follow the simple guidelines they will reduce any risk of infection and of catching AIDS. If a young person is HIV positive or has AIDS they will need extra help and support as well as education on just what it all means and how it will affect them. You may need to get specialist help.

Keeping a health record sheet

Is it a good idea to keep a record of my health care? Yes, because:

- Later in life we are often asked to fill in forms about our medical records and it helps to remember detail.

- Young people can take their records with them if they move somewhere else.

- They may find there is a pattern of regular illness. By looking at their records and thinking what they have done they may be able to work out why.

Carers will have guidelines as to what is required whilst a young person is being looked after:

- They should be offered a health assessment every year and be involved in the formulation of their health care plan following an assessment.

- Their eyes should be tested as necessary.

- Dental check ups are recommended every six months.

Encourage them to continue this when they become independent. There is a health record sheet on pages 63-64 that young people might like to use when they are no longer looked after.

Carers must also keep a record of any medicines the young people have taken or must take.

Drug abuse

Many young people will have experimented with drugs in some form before they leave school.

Why do they do it?

- It's an alternative to alcohol or solvents.
- Young people like the excitement, the element of danger.
- If adults are shocked, that can be an attraction.
- Young people like experimenting with new sensations.
- Hallucinations or sensations can be interesting and exciting.
- Hallucinations can also be dangerous, unpleasant and frightening, but even these can be enjoyable (think of horror films).
- Drugs allow young people to escape – albeit temporarily, and only in their imagination.
- They may be lonely, feel inadequate, lack self-esteem or confidence and think taking drugs will help.
- They think it will help them 'blot out' problems.
- They are encouraged by their friends, or made to look small if they refuse.

 ## What should I look for?

There are often no clear-cut signs, and many of the effects are hard to distinguish from normal growing up. Many teenagers are moody without having taken drugs. Look out for:

- Any sudden change in behaviour or lifestyle, for example, going around with a new set of friends.
- Wide swings in mood or behaviour – depression, lethargy, followed by being outgoing, active or chatty.
- Loss of appetite.
- Being unusually aggressive.
- Being unusually drowsy or sleepy.
- Asking for money from their friends or carers without explaining what it is for or with feeble explanations.
- Loss of money or other objects from the house.
- Secretiveness or lying.
- Unusual stains, marks or smells on the body, or clothes, or around the house.

Don't jump to conclusions, but be alert to the signs.

Watch out also for:

- scorched pieces of tin foil

- a home-made pipe

- the remains of a cannabis cigarette with small cardboard tube filter

- dilated pupils in the eyes

- rash around the mouth

 ## What drugs might they take?

Unfortunately, there are many different drugs available to young people. They include:

- cannabis

- magic mushrooms

- hallucinogens

- amphetamines or speed

- ecstasy

- cocaine

- crack

- heroin

- barbiturates

- benzodiazephines

- solvents

These often have 'street' names which may change with fashion.

Most areas will have places such as youth advisory centres, GP surgeries and schools where the carer or young person can get more details or help if required. There are very good booklets published by the Health Education Authority and other groups. They give facts about the many drugs available including:

- the other names that might be used

- what they look like

- how they are taken

- the effects

- the health risks

- their legal status

The booklets note that the word 'parent' is used as an abbreviation for any adult responsible for a young person. They also note that the term 'drugs' refers both to illegal drugs, prescribed drugs taken inappropriately, and household products which are freely available that can be abused.

Injecting drugs

Many young people will try taking drugs and stop immediately. Sadly, others will not. Injecting drugs can be the most dangerous because of the risks of:

- **Infection** where injecting equipment is unsterile and shared. The most serious infections are HIV (which can develop into AIDS) and hepatitis. If a young person is injecting drugs they may get hepatitis B. Make sure they know the immediate dangers – for example, using the wrong injection methods – and get help for the long term but in the short term make sure they get a supply of clean needles. Sometimes these are available free from Drugs Advisory Centres in your area.

- **Abscesses and thrombosis** and other conditions from injecting drugs that were never intended for injection.

- **Gangrene** from hitting an artery instead of a vein.

- **Blood poisoning** caused by a wound becoming infected.

- **Overdose** when a drug of unknown strength is delivered directly into the bloodstream.

The question of drug abuse should be discussed at planning meetings or reviews where any decisions will be made.

 What can I do if a young person is 'high'?

- Keep calm and be patient – you have got to try to bring them down.

- Talk to them about how they feel at that moment.

- Ask them questions about where they are or what they can see – they may be suffering from hallucinations. One young person said he saw 'pink elephants' but the changes may be more subtle for other young people. The effects will be different for each individual. Sometimes these hallucinations persist even after the person is 'sober' again.

- Gradually, slowly, quietly, explain where they are, who you are.

- Keep talking, don't threaten, be pleasant – the time for punishments (if appropriate) and explanations may be later.

- Sometimes just to leave them to themselves is the best solution but you will need to stay alert.

 What should I do in an emergency?

- Make sure they've got fresh air.

- Turn them on their side so they won't choke on their vomit.

- Don't leave them alone.

- Get someone to dial 999 and ask for an ambulance.

- Collect any powders, tablets or anything else they may have been using and give it all to the paramedics when the ambulance arrives.

How can I help prevent drug abuse?

- Talk to the young people about their views on drugs.

- Help them have new, interesting and challenging experiences.

- Get them to think about how they might refuse drugs without losing their friends.

- Teach them to care for and value their health.

- Help them build up their self-esteem and respect for themselves.

- Treat them with respect.

- Take an interest in their opinions and worries.

- Check out any problems they may have.

Where can I get advice?

Fostering Networks provide a useful leaflet on the subject *Foster Care and Drug Abuse*. There are also many local and national organisations available for advice – Citizens' Advice Bureaux or libraries should be able to help.

Solvent abuse

After smoking and alcohol, **glue sniffing**, as solvent abuse is commonly called, is the most common form of teenage experimentation. Children often start as young as 8-9 years but the peak age is 13-14 years.

What might young people sniff?

- butane gas (in cigarette lighters and refill canisters)

- aerosol sprays including deodorants

- correcting fluids (such as Tipp-Ex)

- solvent-based glues (such as Evo-Stik)

- dry-cleaning fluids

- the contents of some types of fire extinguishers

- thinners

- petrol

- liquid shoe polish

- almost any other household product

Why do they do it?

- It's an alternative to alcohol.
- They like the excitement, the element of danger.
- If adults are shocked, that can be an attraction.
- They like experimenting with new sensations.
- Solvents are cheap and easy to buy or steal!
- Hallucinations when sniffing can be interesting and exciting.
- They may hate themselves and see the possible self-inflicted damage as a motivator.
- Hallucinations can also be dangerous, unpleasant and frightening, but even these can be enjoyable (think of horror films). They allow youngsters to escape – albeit temporarily and only in their imagination.
- They think it will help them 'blot out' problems.
- Peer pressure.
- They may be lonely, feel inadequate, lack self-esteem or confidence.

What should I look for?

There are no clear-cut signs and many of the effects are hard to distinguish from normal growing up. Moodiness may be a result of sniffing but many teenagers are moody without having tried solvents. Signs to watch out for include:

- Finding quantities of empty butane, aerosol or glue cans, or plastic bags in a place where you know young people have been.
- Chemical smell on clothes or breath.
- 'Drunken' behaviour.
- Any sudden change in behaviour or lifestyle, for example, going around with a new set of friends.
- Wide swings in mood or behaviour.
- Spots around nose and mouth (**glue sniffers' rash** only occurs with some glues and may not be as common as acne!) .
- Loss of appetite.
- Asking for money from their friends or carers without explaining what it is for, or with feeble explanations.
- Secretiveness about leisure-time activities.
- Frequent and persistent headaches, sore throat or runny nose – a quick visit to the doctor would be wise.

Don't jump to conclusions, but be alert to the signs.

A young person told us:

> *Solvent abuse is dangerous because the initial 'buzz' only lasts seconds so continual use is needed to keep the high going, which can lead to suffocation.*

 How can I help?

Most young people who try sniffing will only do it a few times and stop without any help from adults. But if you find a young person **has** tried solvents, it is important to deal with it calmly:

- They may not realise that it is dangerous, so telling them of the dangers may be all they need.

- Don't nag or preach, talk to them, show you are concerned, help them to change their ways.

- Be a good listener – perhaps there are problems you don't know about. These problems may be far more important than the sniffing.

- If they have been sniffing for some time, arrange a health check.

- It may be difficult to stop a determined sniffer, so stay alert.

- Arrange other activities together – it will show you care and will give them other things to do. It will also help you to keep track of how they are using their free time.

- Suggest they join a youth club, take part in physical activities or trips out of town – it'll give them a chance to meet new groups of young people.

- For those young people who refuse to stop using solvents you may want to give advice on how to avoid, or reduce damage to their health.

HEALTH RECORD SHEET 1

Name _____   Blood group _____

Name and address of doctor _____

_____

_____

Telephone number _____

Date	Treatment

Date	Type of injection

HEALTH RECORD SHEET 2

Name and address of dentist _____

_____

_____

Telephone number _____

Date	Treatment

Name and address of optician _____

_____

_____

Telephone number _____

Date	Treatment/advice

Section 7
Personal development

Introduction: growing up

Probably the most difficult phase of our lives is our teens. Do you remember having spots, big feet, developing breasts, having greasy hair, wearing clothes that didn't suit you, blushing, having a crush on a teacher?

The following section covers some of the topics young people being looked after have asked for help with. These include:

- making decisions
- discipline and punishment
- privacy and confidentiality
- self-respect, confidence and self-esteem
- values
- listening and being listened to
- coping with crisis
- worries

Provide them with a happy, warm, caring environment where they can talk about worries openly, have their own privacy and entertain their friends and 'those terrible teenage years' will not be so bad at all.

It's nice when all the kids and all the staff get together and have discussions.

I think a good carer is someone who sits down and listens to you...and someone who will follow it through and try to sort out the problem.

People who actually work in children's homes and do all the dirty work. I think they understand.

You can talk to your foster carer and get an honest answer.

The most valuable thing you can give a young person growing up is your time. Time to listen, time to talk, time to communicate, time to understand. Growing up nowadays is particularly difficult; they'll need all the help and support you can give them.

Making decisions

Few people like making decisions. We all know it's much easier to put off making decisions until tomorrow! But decision-making is an important life skill so young people need help in learning how to do it. They also need to learn to make decisions so that when they are no longer being looked after, making decisions will be a natural thing to do. Hopefully young people won't rush into things but look at the situation from every angle, exploring the options, and then decide.

There is pressure on children to make decisions they are not equipped to make.

Foster carer

Let them start with simple decisions at first, like choosing menus, helping choose holidays, outings, subjects at school, colour schemes, even if it is much easier for you to make the decisions yourself.

Here are three ways that could be used to help the decision-making process. You could work through them with the young people on a few minor issues at first. You could use them either with just one young person, or working in a group.

Decision-making methods

1. Simple logical method

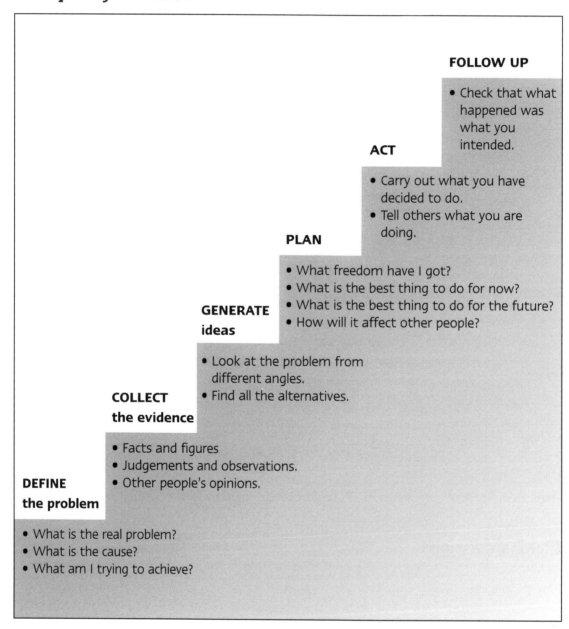

FOLLOW UP

- Check that what happened was what you intended.

ACT

- Carry out what you have decided to do.
- Tell others what you are doing.

PLAN

- What freedom have I got?
- What is the best thing to do for now?
- What is the best thing to do for the future?
- How will it affect other people?

GENERATE ideas

- Look at the problem from different angles.
- Find all the alternatives.

COLLECT the evidence

- Facts and figures
- Judgements and observations.
- Other people's opinions.

DEFINE the problem

- What is the real problem?
- What is the cause?
- What am I trying to achieve?

2. For and against (pros and cons) method

Make a list of all the good points and all the bad points of making a decision, see Figure 7.1 for an example. It is surprising when you have done this how easy the decision will be. If you have more than one choice then you can compare the 'fors' and 'against'.

Choice	For	Against
Staying on at same school in 6th form		
Going to local college		
Going to college in next town		

Figure 7.1: Pros and cons form

3. Rating method

Making decisions using the rating method means that you look at the options and then give each option a value. In this way you can work out what each option really means to you, see Figure 7.2 for an example of a completed Rating Form:

1. Write down the option or choices at the top of the columns marked X, Y, Z. More columns can be added if needed.

2. Write down all the points or factors that you want to consider in the column marked **Requirements**, usually about 10 points.

3. Give the points a mark out of 10 (10 being the most important and 1 the least important). Put these numbers in the column marked **Rating** (a). No number should be used twice in this column. This will show the overall importance to you of the various points.

4. Give X, Y, Z a mark out of 10 to show how well they meet the **Requirements**. Write the mark in column (b). This will show the difference between each option.

5. Multiply the figure in column (a) by the figure in column (b) and put your answer in column (c). Do this for each option.

6. Add up all the scores in each column (c). The highest score will be the best option.

Figure 7.3 is a blank Rating Form which can be photocopied and used again and again.

Of course, it may be that once you start putting a value on the requirements they seem less important and you will want to change them.

REQUIREMENTS	RATING A	Option/choice (all answers out of 10)					
		X Staying on at school in 6th form		Y Going to local college		Z Going to college in next town	
		B	C	B	C	B	C
Choice of subjects	10	7	70	9	90	8	80
Travelling time	4	8	32	5	20	3	12
Travel costs	9	9	81	4	36	8	72
Having friends there	5	10	50	2	10	10	50
Good exam pass rate	8	6	48	8	64	9	72
Good sports facilities	6	10	60	6	36	10	60
Library	2	2	4	3	6	4	8
Good social life	7	3	21	5	35	7	49
Nearness to shops	1	1	1	1	1	3	3
Good canteen	3	1	3	3	9	8	24
Total			370		307		430

Figure 7.2: Example of rating method

REQUIREMENTS	RATING A	Option/choice (all answers out of 10)					
		X		Y		Z	
		B	C	B	C	B	C

Figure 7.3: Rating method form

Encouraging positive behaviour

Behaviour is a way of communicating. With some young people being difficult may be their way, often their only way, of telling you that they feel awful, angry or distressed about something or everything. Extreme behaviour is often related to extreme distress.

When a young person has been particularly difficult, especially if this behaviour comes out of the blue, try to find out what is bothering them – not, of course, until they have calmed down. If the young person is reluctant to talk, you might find the section on *Worries* helpful (page 90).

It is a good idea to make a note of when difficult behaviour occurs to see if there is a pattern. For example, a young person may be 'high' say every Tuesday, after school, because, for example, they 'hate' the teacher of a particular subject. Someone else may be difficult after reviews or visits home. You can then make your own plans of how to prevent problems occurring.

It is also worth noting when the young person is **not** being difficult. You can then speak to them positively and look for ways of lessening the difficult behaviour. This sort of analysis is called the ABC analysis.

    A Antecedent – what happens before the behaviour?

    B Behaviour – what actually happens?

    C Consequence – what happens as a result of the behaviour?

It is equally useful for positive behaviour as well as for difficult behaviour as it helps build a picture of the young person's behaviour patterns and will help you to take action accordingly.

How do I know what I can and can't do?

Young people should be encouraged to discuss:

- Their behaviour and others' behaviour.
- Concepts of right and wrong.
- What is acceptable and what is not.
- What control is needed and why.
- What sanctions should be imposed, how and by whom. They need to believe the system in their home is fair and is applied 'across the board', consistently.
- Their relationship with carers, teachers and other young people and why they might feel aggressive towards them; frightened of them; impressed by them.
- They need to learn to aim for standards they can achieve.
- They need help to find ways to channel their energy and aggression such as taking up a sport, riding their bike or just going for a walk.

> **It is important that the young person learns to be responsible for their own behaviour.**

I want discipline!

At my review I got what I wanted...I had got used to discipline...and there wasn't any. I asked to be disciplined. My brother asked to be disciplined.

Hampshire teenager

Young people really do want discipline. They want to know their carers care. They want to know how far they can go and what the consequences will be if they go beyond the boundaries. In many local authority areas the term **care and control** is used instead of **discipline and punishment** but young people seem to prefer terms they know.

The following forms of **punishment** should not be used:

- Corporal (physical punishment). (Note: it is allowed in Scotland in 'exceptional circumstances').
- Withholding food, drink and medicines from young people.
- Restricting contact with family or social workers.
- Forcing young people to wear clothing that is different or unsuitable.
- Depriving young people of sleep.
- Withholding medical or dental treatment.
- Fines.

With regard to punishment, carers are permitted to enforce 'reasonable' discipline and punishment but they should take the above as guidelines. A good carer will be aware of what is going on in the home and will often be able to diffuse a situation just by being in the room, or in a doorway, or in the garden.

However, if a situation gets out of control or the young person is likely to harm themselves or others, then carers may, in exceptional circumstances, use minimum physical constraint or lock doors to prevent escape. Bedroom doors should not be locked at night although occasionally it may be necessary for the carer to be near the bedroom to ensure the young person does not run away. A record must be kept if physical restraint is used in residential care.

Tips for care and control

- Praise positive behaviour.
- Work hard to build a good relationship with the young person.
- Provide them with a good environment, a home they value. If the place looks good, and the young people are involved in setting the rules and in decisions that affect the home they will behave much better.
- Involve them in tasks and help them complete them, but make sure the tasks are not too difficult and that they understand what is required. When the going gets tough some young people may give up. Help them to see the task through – you'll be surprised how pleased they will be. They'll have a sense of achievement even with the most simple job.
- Find ways to relieve boredom. Look for ways to stimulate young people.
- Don't say 'no' too often but if you do say no, then keep to it.

- Be friendly with the young person. However, they may need to have someone to rebel against and that person will probably be you.
- Young people will need to learn to trust you and to know you will trust them. They want to respect you – their behaviour may not always indicate this. Be patient.
- Try to stay one step ahead of the young person. Plan activities, events, discussions.
- Be ready for possible explosive situations.
- Be around the house, be available for a chat. It's often just as easy for you to carry out tasks away from the kitchen or office.

Talking and listening are the real keys to care and control.

If the young person is very angry or aggressive, then:
- *Don't* have a slanging match.
- *Don't* swear.
- Think about what you say.
- *Don't* shout or stand in an aggressive way.
- Let them be angry. Channel that anger. Let them hit their pillow or whack the mattress. You could even give them a rolled up newspaper to do it!
- If they really are aggressive try to move them to another room for their own safety if necessary.
- **Stay calm at all costs**.
- Wait for the right moment – perhaps when the young person has calmed down – to talk to them.
- Let them know you care.

Later, carry out an **ABC** analysis. It may be something you could do together.

Privacy and confidentiality

As young people grow up they have a wish for secrecy; a desire for privacy and confidentiality. Many parents and carers find this difficult to cope with. This is a very natural part of growing up and should be respected. Young people being looked after often hate the thought that they are talked about or that what they think they have told someone in confidence is being passed to someone else. They also hate to think that their file can easily be read by others.

We all want our privacy to be respected and young people are no different:
- Letters addressed to them should not be opened or read.
- The telephone should be put somewhere so that confidential calls can be taken.
- Friends should be able to come to visit and be seen in private.
- They should have cupboards that can be locked so they can store their own belongings safely.
- Allow them to self-manage an appropriate budget such as the call list and payment for their mobile phones.

Carers and parents alike are no different and like to see things tidy. Yet young people need their own space where they can leave things as they wish knowing they won't be gone through or examined. Sometimes if you were to go through a young person's belongings you might find drawings, writings or pictures you wished you hadn't seen or that will shock you. Usually this is just a normal part of growing up, finding out about their sexuality, or expressing their feelings and emotions. They would possibly 'rather die' than think someone had seen them.

Young people need to know under what circumstances their 'space' will be entered, for example, if it is felt the young person is at risk, or, to clear up the room if it is a health hazard. Carers will also have their own personal belongings – respecting privacy should be a two-way process. Privacy and confidentiality can be a good area for discussion.

Some secrets cannot be kept – if you are worried that a young person has suffered or is likely to suffer 'significant harm', you may have to take the matter further, but the young person needs to know what you intend doing, why, and to be kept informed.

Self-respect, confidence and self-esteem

The teacher said:

> *You are a no-hoper. You'll leave school with nothing.*

The no-hoper is now at college.

Everyone needs to be valued, to feel special, and to feel important. By treating young people looked after as individuals, working and caring for them you will build up their self-confidence. By making opportunities for young people to succeed you will build up their self-esteem.

No matter what difficulties a young person has had in the past, they need to know that you expect them to overcome these difficulties. That they are responsible for their own life and behaviour. Treat them with respect and gradually they will learn to respect you and others around, and also to respect themselves for what they are.

 What other questions might help them do this?

On page 79 is an exercise called *Know Yourself*. Young people might like to do this on their own, with you, or in a group. It may help them to look at things with 'fresh eyes'. If young people show you their answers, you may be surprised, indignant or hurt, but at least you may know the young person a little better. You might also use it as a talking tool. To have self-respect and to build up confidence they have to understand and know themselves, what makes them tick, and realise that they must take responsibility for their own actions.

If it annoys them to answer this 'stupid' questionnaire, you should think about why...

Values

We seem to be bombarded with all sorts of guidance to ensure that young people are helped in all sorts of ways, so that they learn to become responsible caring adults. However, young people still need help to learn to make decisions in their lives.

I want to know right from wrong.

Young person

They need to learn to:

- Know the difference between right and wrong.
- Tell the truth.
- Keep promises.
- Respect the rights and properties of others.
- Act considerately.
- Help those less fortunate and weaker than themselves.
- Take personal responsibility for their actions and self-discipline.

 What does all this mean?

It means that you, as the carer of young people, will need to work with them, to help them develop their own sense of values. They should also be taught to reject:

- bullying
- cheating
- deceit
- cruelty
- discrimination and prejudice – whether due to gender, class, race or sexuality

Many young people complain if someone cheats on them, yet a little later will cheat on others. They need to learn about standards, about what is acceptable and what is not acceptable, and to think about how others feel, and not just think about themselves. As they grow up they will become aware of issues such as:

- damage to the environment
- smoking
- divorce
- loyalty
- drinking alcohol
- blood sports
- abortion
- sexuality

All of these are good topics for discussion. Group discussions, individual discussions, reading newspapers and watching particular television programmes are all ways that can develop a young person's beliefs. Of course, young people will always question why things are as they are and will test the boundaries, but there needs to be boundaries so they know where they stand, so they have something to rebel against, and so that they have something to stand them in good stead for the future.

Young people who self-harm

One of the most difficult situations carers face is when confronted with a young person who deliberately harms themselves. Whether it is a one-off or a regular occurrence, it causes a whole variety of strong feelings, from intense anger through to fear, anxiety and sadness. Caring is about making life better for those in care, so acts of self-harm can lead to feelings of failure and helplessness.

 ## What is self-harm?

We all harm ourselves sometimes, for example, by smoking, drinking, reckless driving, unprotected sex, or simply by not always taking good care of ourselves or our diet. However, self-harm is a deliberate act which inflicts pain or injury to one's own body. It is a way of coping and getting through a bad patch.

 ## How do young people harm themselves?

- Cutting or scratching (arms, legs etc.).
- Banging or bruising.
- Burning.
- Hair pulling.
- Scrubbing with abrasives such as bleach.
- Swallowing harmful substances.

 ## How often does it happen?

As self-harm is often a secretive act it is not possible to know how often it occurs. It can happen once or many times, as a daily response or periodically when a problem arises. Most people who hurt themselves do so quite superficially and carefully. It is only a minority who do so severely and need outside medical treatment for their injuries. Most people stop self-harming when they are ready.

What is the difference between self-harm and attempted suicide?

It is not easy to draw a distinction between self-harm and attempted suicide although it is easy to believe that one would or could lead to the other. Both reflect deep distress but the young person who self-harms is not wishing to kill themselves but deaden the painful feelings they are experiencing. It is an attempt to cope with these painful feelings, yet stay alive.

 ## Why might a young person self-harm?

- To release tension and feelings that have become bottled up inside, hurting so much as to become unbearable. These feelings may stem from current difficulties in life, for example, stress of exams, a break up with a boy or girl friend, racial harassment, confusion about sexual identity or may be a response to past painful experiences, for example, abuse.
- To escape for a while from painful feelings or memories.
- To make their body unattractive so keeping others at bay.
- To gain some control, particularly young people who have been abused and were powerless.
- To punish themselves, so atoning for feelings of being bad or guilty.
- To seek help by demonstrating their distress.
- To comfort themselves – not just the release of tension but also having something 'special' one can do for oneself which may also gain attention and care from others.

 ## How can you help a young person who is self-harming or attempts suicide?

Be prepared. General help may include:
- Be aware of information on the young person's past history of self-harm and/or significant events that might cause distress.
- Reduce their feelings of powerlessness by consulting and acting on their views.
- Don't let their behaviour or the way you deal with it make you lose sight of the young person themselves.
- Give praise.
- Value them.
- Look after them in all ways.
- Provide opportunities for them to talk.

- Show in your daily life that there are other ways of coping with stress and problems.

- Talk with them not at them.

- Actively listen.

- Reduce the need for self-harm, and the harm itself, by offering other options but recognise it may take considerable time and support.

- Encourage and create opportunities to talk, doing so at the young person's pace, in their time and place.

- Encourage other ways of communicating and expressing feelings, for example, through writing letters, keeping a diary, drawing, composing poetry, all of which need not be shared, or you could provide a punchbag or a cushion for them to hit.

- Who else might they feel comfortable talking to?

- Be sympathetic and understanding to the feelings of shame, guilt and confusion the young person may be feeling.

- Provide practical care and comfort – a favourite meal, a pet, a bath.

- Provide basic assistance, for example, a first aid box and simple instructions to the young person – help them to help themselves – it isn't necessarily helpful to step in and do it for them.

Let them feel:

- They are being taken seriously.

- They are supported and that things will be right again.

- A sense of perspective.

- Loved and attached to people who are hurt by their behaviour.

A carer should **not** think:

- They can stop the young person – the young person must **want** to stop. Time and patience is the biggest help the carer can give.

- They are responsible for the action.

- They should make the young person feel guilty.

- Of telling anyone without the young person's consent.

Remember, with help and support things can, and usually do get better, and young people find other ways of sorting out their problems, and dealing with their feelings.

Listening and being listened to

A good communicator should not lie or build up false hopes. They should be trustworthy, reliable and honest, and most especially, a good listener. You cannot listen to young people all the time, but you can often spot those who have something important to say by a change of behaviour or mood.

Some simple listening rules

1. Never be too busy to listen. Young people have important things to say at the most inconvenient time of the day.

2. Listen to what is being said. Give the young person your entire attention.

3. Don't anticipate what will be said next. Wait and listen. That way you'll be sure.

4. Keep your thoughts to yourself as to what is being said. Don't let your mind jump away from the topic.

5. Pay attention to both *what* is being said and *how* it is being said.

6. If you have a question, make a note of it and ask it at the proper time. Don't interrupt or write while the young person is talking. Asking questions can certainly help but they require careful handling and good timing.

7. If you disagree, don't get angry. Wait until they have finished. They may say something that makes your anger unnecessary or even embarrassing.

8. If the young person is continuing for a long time, jot down a few notes. This will help later on in remembering what was said.

Listening is as much an art as speaking

Both require practice

Both require attention

A good listener will usually be listened to because they will have taken care to listen and will have thought about what they want to say. If you want to talk to a young person:

- Plan the time and place to suit both of you and if necessary or possible, tell them in advance. Don't choose a time when their favourite TV programme is on!

- Plan what you want to say.

- Jot down the main points you want to say.

- Have a pen and paper ready to make notes.

- Tell them at the start what you want to discuss.

- End by saying what is agreed and what action is to be taken.

- Don't gossip or pass on what you have heard.

- Show you are listening by your eye contact, nodding or use of body language.

- Respect confidentiality and privacy unless you feel the young person is at risk of significant harm.

If you feel you must pass on something you have been told: tell the young person concerned, explaining:

- The reasons why you are doing this.

- What you will do.

- How you will do it.

- Why you are taking that particular course of action.

- When you will be doing it.

At all times help keep them informed of what is happening. Be honest and never make promises you can't keep.

KNOW YOURSELF CHECKLIST: THE 3-POINTER

3 things you are good at:

1 ....

2 ....

3 ....

3 things you are not so good at:

1 ....

2 ....

3 ....

3 ways you could improve:

1 ....

2 ....

3 ....

3 likes

In food?	In clothes?	School/college work?	Other things you like
1	1	1	1 ....
2	2	2	2 ....
3	3	3	3 ....

3 dislikes

In food?	In clothes?	School/college work?	Other things you dislike
1	1	1	1 ....
2	2	2	2 ....
3	3	3	3 ....

→

What would make you change any of these answers:

....

....

....

The 3 best points about yourself:

1 ....

2 ....

3 ....

The 3 worst points about yourself:

1 ....

2 ....

3 ....

3 ways you could improve on your worst points:

1 ....

2 ....

3 ....

What do you dislike most about other people?

1 ....

2 ....

3 ....

Section 8
forming relationships

Introduction: friendships

I'm 17, going on 40...

What Steve went on to explain was that what he had been through in his life up to the age of 17 was probably as much as many people go through up to the age of 40.

I have nothing in common with anyone who has not been in care.

Again, what he was saying was that he felt that most 17-year-olds had very little else to think about other than clothes, parties and discos: whereas he had to think about rent, bills, food, budgeting etc. as well. If a teenager has been sexually abused, their sexual awareness may be heightened, or the reverse, and they may feel revulsion towards that person or anyone else who reminds them of that person. This often makes it more difficult for young people who have been abused to make or trust new friends.

Young people who are looked after may also have come from difficult backgrounds where they've moved around a lot and not had a chance to make 'best friends'. They may not, therefore, have gone through the usual process of making and keeping friends.

They may also be very lonely so if someone from the opposite sex comes along and gives them some attention they may fall madly in love with them, sometimes to the exclusion of everyone and everything else. This person may also be much older than they are; a mother or father figure; a car owner; someone with plenty of money. Young people who are being looked after may also never have had a loving, caring relationship with an adult.

Carers must come to terms with their own feelings, beliefs and uncertainties before they will be able to openly discuss sex, sexuality and relationships with young people. They may also need to obtain guidance from the local authority as to what is acceptable practice in their region.

Making and keeping friends

Some people find making friends easy: others find it very hard. Some people call someone they have just met 'a friend'. Others use the term with more care. A friend is someone you can trust, who you can talk to and want to spend time with.

How can I make new friends?

Young people can be encouraged to have wide interests, so they will meet all sorts of people – easier said than done, especially when they are in their early teens. Black young people living with white carers may need help to link up with the black community.

As a carer, you can:

- Help young people to build up their self-respect and confidence (see previous section).

- Help young people to understand themselves better, realising that not only is there probably a good reason why they behave in a certain way but also why other people behave the way they do.

One of the hardest lessons to learn for everyone but particularly young people being looked after, is self control – not to lose their temper, to count to 10, to try to look at things from others' points of view, not just their own. The best way to learn is by example. If a relationship is worth having then it's worth maintaining; that sometimes you have to compromise, make allowances, or swallow your pride and say sorry – this goes for adults and young people.

Remember! If in your home young people are used to discussing and talking about all sorts of things and listening to others' points of view this will help them with their friendships. Some big problems encountered by young looked-after people are:

- Moving from a family into group living.
- Moving from group living into:
  - living in a family
  - living on their own
  - living with chosen friends

If they move into a children's home they often give up their friends, and are only friendly with those in the home. This is a real problem when they move out.

- Encourage them to keep their existing friends, and also to make new friends outside the home.

- If it is possible, get them to stay at their friend's house and to go on school or college trips which entail overnight stays.

A new resident in a children's home may find it difficult to cope with the lack of personal attention, the noise, people constantly being around. On the other hand, children's home residents often find the move back home or into foster care difficult to cope with and the closeness hard to handle. Both groups will need help with this change.

The loneliness of living independently is also very hard to cope with for a young person who is used to having people around them all the time and someone to call on in time of need. Make sure they know of all the different points of contact available to help them.

Staying with friends

During their time being looked after by social services, there often seems to be a lot of niggly little rules and regulations that cause discontent amongst young people. Staying with friends is one such set of rules. If you explain the reasons why the rules are there, they may still not like them but at least they will understand.

 Can I go to stay with friends?

Yes, of course young people can, but a carer will need to ask where they are going and who they are going to stay with. You or the young person's social worker will have to find out all you can about the people they want to visit. Parental or guardian permission may be necessary. A police check may also have to be made.

 Why do you have to do this?

While young people are being looked after by social services, a carer must be sure they are safe and well at all times, and that there won't be any problems. Although asking questions about the people they want to visit may be annoying or embarrassing for them, it has to be done to ensure the young person's safety. It also ensures that there won't be people present, whom the young person is not meant to see.

 What happens if I want to baby-sit and stay overnight?

Whatever the reason for staying out overnight, carers will need to know in advance. A young person should not stay out overnight until you have found out about the people the young person wants to stay with.

Personal relationships and sex

Sex should be a normal and healthy part of our lives. As a young person grows up, it is important that they discuss issues about personal relationships and sex with someone they trust. It cannot be assumed that young people have all the necessary facts they need.

 What is happening to my body?

Most young people learn the basic 'facts of life' when they are quite young, say 7 or 8. This is usually a very simple explanation given at school. As they reach puberty, young people need to know about periods, wet dreams, childbirth, as well as about the many physical and emotional changes that occur. Young people in their early teens will have heard all sorts of tales. They may also pretend they know a lot more about sex than they actually do.

Sex is not just about genital contact. It has physical, mental, emotional, individual, social, cultural, religious and political dimensions. The following chart may be helpful in giving some starting points for discussion. This chart is from *Sexuality, Young People and Care* (Bremner and Hillin, 1994). The book also gives useful advice and guidance on such things as attitudes and beliefs of people from different religions or cultures and also helps about ways to work with young people.

Sexual practice Including celibacy	Sexual orientation	Sensuality	Social structures	Political dimensions	Institutional oppressions

	• heterosexual
	• lesbian
	• gay
	• bisexual
	• attraction and desire
		• food
		• sharing meals
		• candlelight
		• clothing
		• fabrics
		• exercise
		• touch
		• massage
		• nature
		• elements:
		  – wind
		  – sun
		  – water
		  – earth
		  – heat
		  – cool
		  – ice
		• aromas, oils
		• intimacy
		• sharing secrets
		• dreams
		• fantasy
		• dance
		• art
		• music
			• marriage
			• living together
			• wedding rings
			• conditioning
			• gender stereotypes
			• dress and grooming
			• rites of passage etc.:
			  – circumcision
			  – bar mitzvah
			  – retreats
			  – first menstruation
			  – tampons
			  – sexual experience
			  – sex education
			• dating
			• going steady
			• engagement
				• feminism
				• women's groups
				• lesbian and gay groups
				• demonstrations
				• celebrations
				• mothers and toddlers groups
				• black groups
				• elders groups
					• oppressions, including:
					  – sexism
					  – racism
					  – heterosexism
					  – ableism
					  – ageism
					  – class etc.
					• institutionalised legal system
					• age of consent
					• medical system
					• mental health
					• equal opportunity programme

Figure 8: Things young people might want to know about

Sex and the law

1. **It is illegal for anyone (male or female) to have sexual intercourse with someone of the opposite sex who is under 16 years of age *even if they agree*.** Attitudes have changed on this in recent times and prosecutions are less likely than in the past.

2. **Female homosexuality is not an offence; however, if either party is under 16 it can be classed as an indecent assault.** The whole question of consent and the law in same-sex relationships is currently under review. CAB, the local library, or the local sexual health clinic should be able to provide the latest information.

3. **Rape** occurs when one person forces another person to have sex without their consent. Rape is a very serious offence. The need to give consent (agreement) is there because people have the right to say 'No'. Even when two people are married, if the woman does not consent to have sexual intercourse, this is an offence of rape.

4. **Indecent exposure** is where someone exposes themselves to someone else in what is considered an unacceptable fashion, in a public place, for example, if a man exposes his penis or buttocks.

5. **Carers, whether residential or foster carers, must not have a sexual relationship of any sort with someone for whom they are caring.**

 What if someone is doing something to me that I do not like?

Young people need to know that they have the right to say NO. **No-one should force another person to have sex.** Everyone's body is their own and they should not be persuaded to do something sexual they do not like, feel unready for or that makes them feel unsafe. If someone forces another person to have sex, that person is committing a serious criminal offence. If anyone tries to kiss a young person or touches them in a way that worries them, the young person should say so and tell someone they trust.

 What should I think about before I have a sexual relationship?

*   'Do I care for and trust this person very much?'
*   'Do they really care about me?'
*   'Am I ready to take on the responsibility of a sexual relationship?'
*   'Will having sex with this person at this time lead to anyone getting hurt?'
*   'Can my partner and I talk openly and honestly about safer sex and birth control?'
*   'Is there anything in my culture or religion that says sex outside marriage is wrong?'
*   'Am I being pressurised into having sex by my partner or friends?'

When do I know I'm ready to have sex?

People often break up with their girl or boyfriends quite soon. It is a normal part of growing up and living, but it can be extremely upsetting. That's why having sex before a young person has a long-term relationship, and a real commitment can lead to someone getting hurt. Feeling sexual and wanting to have sex is natural. Deciding to have sex means being responsible and being prepared to handle the consequences.

But everybody does it?

Deciding not to have sex with someone is a responsible choice. No one should have sex just because their friends say they do it. Anyway, many young people exaggerate about their relationships. Sex is only enjoyable when both partners feel right about it.

What is 'safe sex'?

There is no such thing as 'safe sex', only *safer* sex. Apart from the risk of pregnancy, there is the added worry of AIDS (see HIV/AIDS page 55) and other sexually transmitted diseases.

Limiting the risk of infection

The risk of infection through sex can be limited in a number of ways; by:

- **Not having sex**. If anyone thinks they, or their partner, has an infection (often you can't tell). Be open and frank about it. If anyone thinks they have a sexually transmitted infection they should straight away go to their doctor or to a special clinic, sometimes called a GU or genito-urinary clinic. The address will be in the local telephone directory.

- **Limiting the number of partners**. The more partners a person has the greater the risk of getting an infection.

- **Using a BSI approved condom properly**. To protect one another is an important part of safer sex. It also helps prevent a girl getting pregnant. Condoms can be bought from garages, chemists, machines in toilets, in grocery stores, in fact virtually anywhere. They can be obtained free of charge from local family planning clinics. Condoms are available for men and women.

- **Passing urine and washing their sexual parts as soon as possible after sex**. This may help prevent passing on an infection, and also helps to prevent conditions such as cystitis (a urinary tract infection) and 'thrush' (a fungal infection).

- **Not having sex if they are drunk**. They may either forget to use a condom altogether or may not use it properly.

Pregnancy

Some myths about pregnancy

Contrary to popular rumours, a girl or woman *can* get pregnant:

- The first time she has sex.
- Even before her first period.
- Even if she has a period at the time.
- Whatever position is used.
- Even if she only gets semen near her vagina without having full intercourse at all.

When a man and woman, or a girl and a boy, have sex they risk starting a baby. A baby can totally change the pattern of everyone's lives. That is why young people need to know about contraception (see page 54). Emergency contraception is available up to 72 hours after unprotected sex. It is available from a GP, sexual health clinic, accident and emergency sections of hospital and from some chemists (chemists may charge a fee).

How do I know whether or not I am pregnant?

Young women need to know that if they have been sexually active, and then miss a period, or their period is late, this could mean they are pregnant. If they are worried that they may be pregnant they can find out within days of having sex by having a pregnancy test. They can go to their doctor, sexual health clinic, some youth drop-in clinics or buy a pregnancy test kit from the local chemist. Doing the test themselves may not be 100% reliable, especially if they do not follow the instructions carefully.

What about termination?

If a young woman becomes pregnant and wishes to have an abortion she can contact her own doctor, the local sexual health clinic or the BPAS (British Pregnancy Advisory Service) which gives confidential advice and counselling. It is very important that she seeks help as soon as possible.

On the other hand, the young woman may wish to keep the baby when it is born. Counselling and practical help will be needed. Many local health authorities have specially trained staff to give this sort of help.

What if I get a girl pregnant?

The man is equally responsible for a woman's pregnancy. He also has a responsibility to maintain the child until it is 18 years of age.

Am I legally responsible for the child?

The Child Support Act 1991 says that parents have a legal responsibility to financially maintain any children they have, unless the child is adopted. This applies equally to both parents. Absent parents can have deductions taken directly from their wages until that child is 18 years old to pay for the child's keep.

Sexuality

Television, films and magazines often exploit sexuality in order to increase audience figures. Young people see sex and sexuality as the only thing that matters if they are to have a successful relationship with someone. It really is important that young people learn about all aspects of sexuality and are confident to discuss things openly.

 ## Why should we talk about sex?

Sex, sexuality and relationships are important issues for discussion. During these discussions, the whole question of relationships can be brought up. This will throw up other fundamental things about relationships:

- The value of respecting others and respecting themselves.
- Not having sex with just anyone because it seems a good idea at the time.
- When they meet someone who really means something to them they need to consider carefully whether they are both prepared for the responsibility of having sex.
- Sex is a lot more complicated than just a matter of feelings. It involves health, happiness and freedom.

 ## Am I gay?

Young people may have sexual feelings for someone of the same sex. This does not automatically make them gay. If they feel they are, or if they are unsure, they will need positive and non-judgmental support. There are groups/helplines offering help and support for young lesbians and gays, both nationally and locally. If you feel you cannot help a young person regarding sexual orientation, there should be well-trained counsellors in your area who can help.

 ## Can disabled people have sexual relationships?

Disabled young people have the same feelings and concerns as non-disabled young people. However, they may have a harder time in dealing with them because society often portrays disabled people as non-sexual. Very little information on sexual matters is aimed at disabled people, so it is important they have someone they trust to discuss issues with them. This might be someone from the disability social services team, or a member of the sexual health and relationship team, if you are unable to help.

Section 9
Coping with crisis

Introduction: expressing pain

We are all different, and we all have our different ways of coping with crisis. Some young people will wail and cry so you'll know they have a problem, others will bottle it up. Their unhappiness may show up in health problems. Physical symptoms may include:

- feeling their heart is beating quickly
- pains and tightness in their chest
- indigestion and wind
- colicky stomach pains and diarrhoea
- frequent passing of urine
- tingling feelings in the arms and legs
- muscle tension, often pain in the neck or low part of the back
- persistent headaches
- migraine
- skin rashes
- difficulty focusing the eyes
- lack of self care or poor hygiene

Psychological symptoms may include:

- unreasonable complaints
- withdrawal and daydreams
- missing school or college
- accident-proneness and carelessness
- poor work, cheating and evasion
- starting smoking
- drinking alcohol
- trying out drugs
- over-eating or loss of appetite
- difficulty getting to sleep and waking up tired
- feelings of tiredness and lack of concentration
- irritability

Unfortunately many of these may be just normal growing-up symptoms but if they persist then you may find the young person has a problem.

Some tips to help them cope

- Let them know you care.
- Be available.
- Be a good listener.
- Reassure them.
- Suggest positive steps such as:
  - talking to their friend, teacher or relative
  - taking part in a physical activity
  - giving themselves a treat
- Make them feel secure.
- Help them become independent.
- Help them to look at things from all sides.
- Get them to have a medical check-up. Many problems vanish when they find they've nothing physically wrong with them.
- If it's an emotional crisis, help them to cry.
- Have somewhere private so they can talk or cry without being heard or interrupted.

Worries

A friend of mine has a problem... or I know someone who...

If a young person starts a conversation like that, that 'someone' is often them. All the time they can talk as someone else, they won't get emotionally involved, they don't have to admit they have a problem and also, they can go away and think about what you say without feeling under pressure.

Follow up quite soon by asking 'what happened?' or 'has your friend?' You'll usually be told the truth then. If the matter is serious, get someone else to approach them if you feel you can't get any further or suggest they get in touch with someone they can trust.

We are all different and respond to people differently. Don't be upset if your young person tells their worries to someone else. Very few children are completely open with their own parents, preferring to talk to someone less closely involved with them, be it brother or sister, gran, neighbours, friend or teacher.

Something you and most of the world think is unimportant may be really distressing to a sensitive young person:

- be aware
- be concerned
- be patient
- be available
- be tolerant
- be understanding
- be honest
- be discreet

At the end of this section is a *Worries Checklist*, a list of problems many teenagers said had worried them at some stage. Young people may like to go through the list and put a tick which says how they feel about things at the moment. They can, of course, do this questionnaire in confidence, but if they share it with you you'll get a pretty good idea how you can help. Either way, talking and listening is the best tool for relieving worries.

We all know that even the slightest worry can build up out of all proportion. A minor illness can be blown up to seem like a major life-threatening disease if there is no one on hand to share that worry with. One young lad, who became aggressive and whose school work was suffering, admitted that he thought he had cancer of the testicles. A quick visit to the doctor soon put his mind at rest.

Writing down their worries, both the facts, the situation as they see it and what can be done about it will often help. If they do it with you, you can share their worries and help them overcome them. If they can't talk to you, suggest other people who might help – teacher, social worker, relative, and friend. Talking really is the best tool to relieve worries.

Abuse

Young people who are looked after may have been abused in one form or another at some time in their life. Sadly, this may also occur during their time 'being looked after'.

Sometimes when a young person moves away from the parental home, their circumstances change or something happens to trigger bad memories; previous abuse may be revealed. A carer needs to be alert at all times and have an action plan ready.

 What is abuse?

The main forms of abuse are **physical abuse**, **sexual abuse**, **neglect** and **emotional abuse**.

Physical abuse

There are many kinds of physical abuse. It may be that young people are physically hurt or injured; given poisonous substances or drugs, or imprisoned in some way. Many young people who are physically abused have visible injuries, for example bruises in places that do not normally get bruised by accident; and/or bruises of different ages; marks from beating; black eyes; burns or scalds, unexplained fractures and head injuries.

Physical abuse should be suspected where the explanation of the injury does not fit the facts; or if the young person is reluctant to say how the injury happened, or to explain where they have been and why.

Sexual abuse

Sexual abuse is where young people are exploited to meet the sexual needs of others, and forced or encouraged to perform sexual acts for which they may not be ready, physically or emotionally. This may be fondling, masturbation, oral sex, sexual intercourse, anal intercourse and exposure to pornographic material, including videos.

Common signs of sexual abuse are:

- Injuries or soreness in sexual areas and/or mouth
- A wide range of emotional problems (see below).
- Inappropriate sexual behaviour – overly sexual or extreme fear of intimate contact.
- Knowledge and understanding of sexual matters beyond their age.
- Urinary tract infections.

Neglect

Neglect is a term used to describe the failure of a parent or carer to meet a young person's basic needs, such as providing food, warmth, medical care, shelter.

Emotional abuse

Emotional abuse is where young people suffer as a result of a constant lack of affection, verbal attacks, bullying, racial and other forms of harassment, which undermine a young person's confidence and self-esteem.

 What are the signs of abuse?

Any of the following may be associated with abuse or may be symptoms of distress:

- Poor or deteriorating school or college work.
- Erratic attendance, at school or college.
- Young person's reluctance to go to school or college, or frequent early morning minor illnesses.
- Problems with sleeping, nightmares.
- Complaints of hunger, lack of energy, apathy.
- Possessions often 'lost', dirtied, destroyed.
- Desire to stay around adults or avoid adults, either generally or specifically.
- Reluctance to attend medicals.
- Being unhappy, withdrawn or isolated.
- Having a new tendency to stammer.
- Changes in eating habits, ranging from tummy aches, a lack of appetite, or excessive 'comfort eating' to more serious conditions, such as anorexia, or bulimia.
- Aggression.
- Constant attention-seeking, over-pleasing/compliant behaviour.
- Indications of alcohol, drug or substance abuse.
- Attempted suicide.
- Running away from home.
- Low self-esteem.
- Poor hygiene.
- Finally, unlikely excuses to explain any of the above signs, or refusing to give any reasons for the above.

What are the long-term effects?

Physical scars heal but many young people take longer to recover from the emotional trauma of physical and sexual abuse. They may need professional help. Young people who have been sexually abused over a long period of time may have little understanding of what is appropriate sexual behaviour. This will have to be learnt. Carers must be aware of this and ensure that they do not place themselves in situations which could be misinterpreted.

 ## What happens if a carer suspects abuse?

Where carers are concerned that a child has been abused, they should record their concern, share their concern with a senior staff member and consult their child protection procedures. In some cases they may have to speak to someone outside their own organisation. Breaking confidentiality is a big problem as some young people will tell you, begging you not to tell anyone else. If you have evidence that a young person is being abused then you must pass this on. You will have to explain this to the young person. They'll hate you at first but will be relieved when they know that something is being done. Keep them informed.

 ## How can carers help young people who may have been abused?

Carers can help by:

- Listening to what a young person says.
- Avoiding asking too many questions or asking for unnecessary detail.
- Being alert and observant.
- Protecting the young person.
- Trying to find out what a young person is afraid of.
- Where a young person is in danger of serious harm, following the procedures for protecting the young person.
- Telling the young person what you are going to do and what will happen next.
- Never telling lies to the young person.

 ## Who are the abusers?

Most young people who have been abused are abused by those they know and even like or love – older friends, parents, relatives, carers, neighbours. Often the abuser is also the most caring person in their life. This is particularly difficult for the young person to cope with as they do not want to cause a problem to those close to them but that person may go on to abuse others. You will have to help young people to understand that what abusers do is wrong, that the young person is not to blame, but that everyone must be protected from the abuser.

What are a young person's rights?

Young people are entitled to be protected from all forms of abuse. Let them know they are not alone and that you are there to protect them. Many young people will find it hard to talk about being abused. Others may disclose abuse and then retract their allegations because they think it is too difficult to face up to the consequences. Young people need to know:

- That you can be trusted.
- That you will believe them.
- That they are not to blame.
- That some 'secrets' cannot be kept.

What happens if I report abuse?

When it is suspected a young person has been a victim of abuse, they may be asked to be interviewed at a special safe place by trained staff, one of whom may be from the police. A video or tape recording may be made of this interview, so the young person doesn't have to keep repeating their experiences. A young person may refuse to give an interview. The young person may be asked to have a medical but they may refuse providing the young person has sufficient understanding to make an informed choice. Check your local Child Protection Procedures for further details.

Bullying

Many young people suffer really badly because they are **bullied**. Young people who are bullied are entitled to be protected. They often don't tell anyone in case they are thought of as 'grassers'. Many of the effects of abuse mentioned previously may apply equally to a young person who is being bullied, so carers need to be observant. Studies show that over half of all young people say they have been bullied at some time.

What can I do if I am being bullied?

The following suggestions may help young people who have been bullied. You may like to pass these on or use them as a basis for discussion:

- Suggest the young person gets help, talks to someone they can trust such as their social worker, carer or someone at school.
- If they are worried that telling will make matters worse, let them know that you will be discreet.
- If it doesn't get sorted straight away, tell them not to give up. All schools and colleges should have an 'anti-bullying' policy so schools and colleges need to know what is going on.

What else can I do?

Tips for young people being bullied:

1. Don't let bullies think they are scaring you. Try to ignore or laugh at what they say – it's hard but worth a go.

2. If you do get angry and realise it would have been better staying calm, don't let it show. Walk away as soon as you can.

3. Stay with a crowd – bullies usually pick on you when you're on your own.

4. Keep a diary. Write down what happens each time you are bullied, what is said, when and where. Give this information to those who are helping you.

5. Take up self defence! This doesn't mean 'fighting back', but it will make you feel more confident. Ask about self defence classes where you live.

> **No-one should tolerate bullying and carers need to make it clear that bullies have no place in their home.**

Loss and bereavement

In this section, we have focused on **bereavement**. Bereavement is the experience of those who are left after the death. Children in care may be more likely to hear about the death of someone they know than other children and may not be alongside the person when they die (Francis Sheldon, University of Southampton) so it is important carers are prepared and able to help.

The young person may have regrets about not saying goodbye, about not attending the funeral, about things they said to the person or even about the thoughts and feelings that they had for them. They will need help to close that door; to find another way. The power of symbolism can be very important.

> *My own father re-married and my step-mother did not wish to have anything to do with my sister and me. When he died she made it clear that she did not wish us to attend the funeral and as I had no wish to cause an argument I did not attend. I spent the day of the funeral in a state of limbo, not able to settle or knowing what to do. Eventually, my husband suggested that I should buy a rose bush to plant in our garden in memory of my father. We bought a bush and chose 'Peace' rose which had been my mother's favourite when she was alive. The amazing thing was that once we had planted the rose I felt totally calm and at peace with myself.*

Although such symbolism may not be possible for a young person, what will be helpful is finding a way of demonstrating, acknowledging and remembering the death and life of the person.

On hearing the news of the loss of someone they know and love, a young person will experience many feelings, such as a sense of shock and disbelief, a numbness. This may be followed by:

- misery
- anger
- questioning
- sadness
- self-blame
- blaming others

If a young person knows in advance that the loss is to occur, they will have time to prepare themselves mentally. The impact of the loss is much greater if the loss is sudden. Different young people react to death in different ways. They may:

- cry
- go for long walks alone
- hide in a crowd
- be angry
- eat too much or too little
- smoke or drink alcohol to excess

Let them find their own way. When the time is right, talk to them or let them talk to you. In a society which is, at the same time, multi-cultural, multi-faith, completely without faith, explanations about death are many and varied. Books such as *Concise Guides to Customs of Minority Ethnic Religions* (Collins et al, 1993) may be useful when talking about death, although the book does not cover the Christian religions.

 ## How does talking help?

- It can dispel wrong ideas.
- It helps to make good sense of the loss.
- It helps to lift the burden of responsibility that many young people will feel. For example, if there was a car crash, and they survived, and their mother didn't, they would feel guilt. If they were out enjoying themselves at a party when their father died, they will say 'if only...'

Sometimes this burden may be realistic, and they will need help to come to terms with this. If the person who has died was the abuser, memories may come flooding back. There may be renewed questioning, re-awakening of feeling, unsettled emotions and much of the previous work with the abused young person may need to be repeated.

How long will it take to get over it?

Young people will feel pain: let them. Don't try to make them get over it too quickly. There is no set time that bereavement lasts. They will feel desolation and despair. They may feel there is no sweetness, no purpose, and no point in their lives.

Who am I?...What does it mean for me?...I'm an orphan.

...may be said many times.

The pain will recur again and again – at birthdays, anniversaries, at Christmas, at holiday times and at other times that were special for the particular family. There are times in their life when the loss may be re-experienced such as weddings, the birth of their child, leaving school. Life moves on and the young person will adapt and adjust, but bereavement is never fully dealt with. Help them find practical things they can do, such as collecting mementos or photographs or writing down how they feel.

WORRIES CHECKLIST	✓	✓	✓
Here is a list of other teenagers worries	**This is a problem for me at the moment**		
	Yes	**Sometimes**	**No**
Having to go everywhere with adults.	☐	☐	☐
The neighbours are too nosey, they talk about me.	☐	☐	☐
I feel there are too many people bullying me.	☐	☐	☐
I worry about not having enough skills to earn my living.	☐	☐	☐
Thinking that nobody will fancy me.	☐	☐	☐
People my age not liking me.	☐	☐	☐
I don't know what I can do when I go to work.	☐	☐	☐
I may fail my exams.	☐	☐	☐
I feel all mixed up about life.	☐	☐	☐
I have no-one to help me with my troubles.	☐	☐	☐
I worry friends might turn against me.	☐	☐	☐
I am not as clever as I would like to be.	☐	☐	☐
Is there any point in living?	☐	☐	☐
I have too many arguments.	☐	☐	☐
Grown-ups are always complaining about me.	☐	☐	☐
I have to go to court.	☐	☐	☐
I stay off school, college, work too much.	☐	☐	☐
Teachers, tutors not minding their own business.	☐	☐	☐
My body is not well developed.	☐	☐	☐
I may get pregnant, or get someone else pregnant.	☐	☐	☐
Having to be at home by a certain time.	☐	☐	☐
Wondering why people aren't nicer to me.	☐	☐	☐
Will I be able to do my job well?	☐	☐	☐
People talking about me behind my back.	☐	☐	☐
Having no privacy.	☐	☐	☐
I might be going mad.	☐	☐	☐
I'm not strong enough.	☐	☐	☐
I'm too fat.	☐	☐	☐
I don't know how to say 'No'.	☐	☐	☐

→

	This is a problem for me at the moment		
	Yes	Sometimes	No
Not feeling very clean.	❏	❏	❏
Being bored at school, college.	❏	❏	❏
Not being allowed to pick my own friends.	❏	❏	❏
Being 'in care' – what do people think?	❏	❏	❏
What shall I tell them?	❏	❏	❏
I might not get a job.	❏	❏	❏
Nobody seems to understand me.	❏	❏	❏
Not being trusted.	❏	❏	❏
Telling lies.	❏	❏	❏
I am not allowed to go places where I enjoy myself.	❏	❏	❏
Having to wear school uniform or out-dated clothes.	❏	❏	❏
Tough kids always picking on me.	❏	❏	❏
I need advice about which subjects to take for exams.	❏	❏	❏
Wondering if I will know when I am in love.	❏	❏	❏
Making a fool of myself in front of friends.	❏	❏	❏
Do people think I've done something wrong because I'm 'in care'?	❏	❏	❏
Thinking there won't be any jobs.	❏	❏	❏
Not good at sport.	❏	❏	❏
Being told off too much.	❏	❏	❏
Having too many headaches.	❏	❏	❏
I am not looking good.	❏	❏	❏
Not getting a chance to say what I mean.	❏	❏	❏
Having to keep secrets.	❏	❏	❏
I am not sleeping well.	❏	❏	❏
Being picked on by teachers, tutors.	❏	❏	❏
I am not able to talk to adults.	❏	❏	❏
Not being allowed to bring certain friends back.	❏	❏	❏
Having too many accidents happening to me.	❏	❏	❏
Getting the blame for things I haven't done.	❏	❏	❏
Not knowing what to say when out with people.	❏	❏	❏
No-one cares.	❏	❏	❏

Introduction: after care - a young person's view

Today's care leavers are tomorrow's citizens and parents. An 18-year-old who had recently left care was asked what she thought should be provided for care leavers. Although the list below was written several years ago many young people are still not getting the help and support they deserve. This list, therefore, still applies. It is exactly what she wrote down in no particular order, just as it came to her:

- There should be hostels and flatlets with a live-in warden. Normal renting rules should apply: interview, deposit, contract etc. It should be available to everyone.
- There should be consistent aftercare advice for all and help.
- There should be drop-in centres at the children's home on certain nights or in an emergency.
- There should be a proper meeting before you leave care with your social worker, carer, possibly parents and the young person to discuss all the arrangements. This should include an aftercare booklet.
- There should be a full back-up system if things don't work out. This should be settled before you leave.
- Social services should check your living accommodation fully.
- Moving out should be a gradual process.
- Plans should be made so that young people who have recently left care and who have nowhere to go, have somewhere they can drop in for Christmas.
- There needs to be a helpline for everyday matters.
- There needs to be a list of people who are willing to listen and give advice, i.e. education, careers, money, sexual, religion, culture etc.
- There should be an emergency 24-hour line for problems – drugs, suicide, sexual, family affairs.
- There should be an emergency refuge where they can get you in touch with someone to talk to or a place to stay temporarily.

Preparation and planning

 What will happen to me when I am 16?

This is the most common worry young people in 'care' have. They see news coverage about homeless young people and worry that it might turn out to be them. Young people need you to talk about and plan their future with them. You are the best person to help them and you cannot start too soon. There is a checklist at the end of this section that they might like to use.

Young people will need:

- **Life skills**, like coping with crisis, and making and keeping new friends.
- **Money skills**, like budgeting, saving, filling in social security forms.
- **Practical skills**, like changing a plug, cooking, and cleaning.

 ## When can I stop being looked after by social services?

- When the young person, their carers, their social worker and those with parental responsibility think they are ready.
- If the young person is on a care order, when the court decides the young person no longer needs to be looked after by social services.
- When a young person is 18.

 ## Will I still be able to contact social services?

Yes, social services must give advice and help young people aged between 16 and 21 who have been looked after.

 ## Do I have to become independent?

Yes, a time will come when the young person will find it difficult to live by the rules of the children's home or their carer's home. They will probably want to leave when they reach 18, although some young people start living independently as young as 16.

 ## Will I still be able to go back to visit?

Yes, most children's homes and foster carers will welcome young people back for visits. It may be possible for them to stay overnight.

Some young people find becoming independent a really big problem and need to go back to their previous home. Of course you should welcome them.

Making a plan

 ## Will I get help to prepare for becoming independent?

Yes. A **joint plan** should be drawn up between the young person, the carer, their social worker, if they have one, and other interested parties such as their school, a leaving-care worker, personal adviser, the housing department or health authority.

The plan should show:

- What they are going to do when they become independent.
- Where they are going to live.
- What help they will receive.
- Who will help them.
- What happens if things go wrong.
- How they will manage financially (see pages 33-38).

Everyone involved should be given a copy of the joint plan.

You could also encourage them young person to join a national leaving-care group of other similar young people or join or form a local group, so they can support each other.

 ## Will I get any money to help me buy what I need?

Social services have a special 'one-off' allowance that should be given. Most young people are entitled to this. Make sure they get what they are entitled to. If they stay in full-time education they can receive financial support from social services until they are 21 years old. If, after being independent, they decide to study, they may still be entitled to an allowance. They should ask social services about this.

Normally, Citizens Advice Bureaux, Welfare Advice Centres, Housing Associations, the Department of Social Security or Leaving Care Teams will tell them of any money they might get. Most telephone numbers will be in the 'phone book. Help them to get as much money as they are entitled to.

The most important thing they will need is reassurance. It will be a very big step for them:

- Arm them with all the facts you can.
- Help them get all their allowances.
- Let them know that someone cares.
- Tell them that there will always be someone to turn to in time of need.

Young people who have been looked after are entitled to support by the local authority after they become independent. They are also entitled to information on what help is available.

Training

Many local authorities provide training courses to help young people cope with the problems of leaving care. What young people often need most is help in coping with the emotional side of things – that is where you come in! There are also many courses to help carers prepare young people to become independent.

Housing

When a young person is ready to leave care their choice of what sort of place to get will depend largely on where they want to live.

 Where can I live?

Young people usually say they're going to get a flat or stay with friends. Both of these are often much more difficult than they realise. Although staying with friends can be useful while they are getting themselves sorted out and costs little or no money, it may mean sleeping on the floor, having no privacy and losing their friends if they stay too long! Their friends may also lose any benefits their friends are entitled to as well. Not only is renting a flat very expensive it can also be very lonely if a young person is on their own.

Other choices they might think about are:

- Going back to live with family or relatives.
- Finding lodgings in someone's house.
- Sharing a house or flat with other people.
- Finding a bedsit.
- Living in a hostel.
- Finding bed and breakfast accommodation (but only as a last resort).
- Supported lodgings if they are available.

 What should I think about?

Young people need to:

- Think about the good points and bad points of each.
- Make a list of what would be their ideal.
- Make another list of what they would accept.

Then you or the leaving care person can go about helping them find a suitable place.

 How do I find a place to live?

Local social services departments have a duty to help any young person who has been 'in care'. This may mean helping them find appropriate accommodation. There may be someone specially appointed for this task or you and the young person can do it together. Together you could try:

- Looking in local papers and adverts in shop windows.
- Putting an advert in a shop window or at a community centre.

- Accommodation agencies – they may ask for a deposit and a fee for finding accommodation.

- Council housing department – they have long waiting lists and may not be able to help until the young person is 18. They may have a list of bed and breakfast accommodation and housing co-operatives and housing associations. Let the housing department know all the relevant information about their particular needs as they have certain responsibilities to young people who have been looked after.

- Housing co-operatives provide cheap housing for members. Members sort out rent, choose new members, maintain and repair the accommodation.

- Housing associations manage and sometimes build housing for particular groups of people. They are in close contact with local advice agencies who refer people to them.

Careers

Some young people will already have an idea of what they think they want to be, be it a hairdresser, a nurse, a footballer or a builder or whatever. They will need help to look at all the options.

Many schools and colleges offer young people the chance to take part in a work experience programme. Encourage everyone to take part. It can be a good way of finding out – or making sure of – what they do, and don't want to do.

Try also to get them to think of the longer term rather than to think only of the present and of just getting any old job. The money they get initially might be good, but probably won't improve much in the future when they have other commitments.

Many young people think of the government's training schemes as slave labour, and in a few cases this may be true. But it is not usually the case, and it gives them an opportunity to learn new skills and obtain qualifications. Discourage them from turning down this option out of hand. Try to get them to think about it first. You could also visit the scheme with the young person.

Some young people feel that employers see a stigma attached to those who are 'in care'. Prepare them in case they come across this. Give them help and advice on how to handle the situation. Help them to have an answer ready in case they are asked 'Why?'

Careers Advisory Service

Local authorities must by law provide a careers advisory service although the title may vary across the UK. What is available will also vary from area to area. Most authorities provide an extra allowance so that young people being looked after can be given special help if they need it.

Must I go to their office?

The careers centres will welcome both carers and young people and give help and advice not just on what jobs are available but also on:

- opportunities in further education
- opportunities in training
- schemes for young people
- voluntary work
- career preparation and planning
- counselling and vocational guidance

In fact, they offer all kinds of information, support and help for a young person taking the next step in life. They will also have specialist information for black young people. Interpreters may be provided for young people whose first language is not English. Young people with disabilities should also receive any additional help needed. Occasionally someone from the careers service may be willing to come to work with the young people in their own environment, say in the children's home. Whatever the circumstances, find out what is available and try to get young people to make the best use of it.

Getting a job

Helping a young person to choose a job, and actually get it, requires skill and patience. Although many schools and colleges give very good advice, often a young person will listen to the person closest to them – you. Here are some things to think about and some hints for getting a job.

What kind of job do I want?

Do you want:

- A manual job or an office job?
- To work on your own or with other people?
- To work indoors or outdoors?
- A job where you dress smartly or where you can wear casual clothes all the time?

Do you mind working evenings, weekends or shifts?

How do I find the right job?

- Use your school/college careers service. They may have a questionnaire you can fill in to help you to decide. They will also help you to use their library system to choose a suitable job.
- Talk to as many different people as you can, not just careers advisers or careers teachers.
- Don't just think about one type of job but collect information about others that might suit you.

When you have some ideas about what you want to do, find out:

- What the job involves.
- What qualifications you need.
- What qualifications you will get whilst working.
- What training you will be given.
- What the prospects are for promotion or moving on.

 ## How do I find a job?

Careers offices

These are one of the best sources of local jobs for young people.

Local papers

If you can, get hold of the local papers from neighbouring areas as well.

National papers

Some vacancies for school leavers are advertised in the national press. Public libraries have copies of many newspapers which can be read every day. It will save buying them and save money.

Job centres

Many types of jobs are advertised here. If you can't see what you want, ask.

Employment agencies

If you have work experience or a skill, such as typing, agencies may take you onto their books.

Personal contacts

Ask friends and relatives to keep their eyes open and tell you about any suitable vacancies that come up.

The internet

Many schools will have access to the internet for job searching, or you can do it at home.

When jobs are not easy to find it is especially important you take a lot of care with your applications.

How do I apply for a job?

If you see an advert in a local or national paper, the advert you see may tell you your next step which may be:

- Ring for an application form.

- Write for an application form.

- Ring saying why you feel you could do the job.

- Write saying why you feel you could do the job.

- Write saying why you feel you could do the job and enclose a cv (see page 110).

If the advertisement tells you to 'Write for an application form' then it means do not telephone. Your letter may however be typed or printed from a computer. If it says 'Apply in your own hand writing' then it must not be typed.

If you see a job advertised that you think you would like, and could do, but do not have the qualifications, then write and tell them about yourself, explaining exactly what you have to offer.

It may be that the qualifications asked for are only a guideline. It may be the employer is confused about the different qualifications. This happened recently when a job was advertised asking for 'A' level maths. When the careers teacher telephoned and explained details of 'A' level maths the company soon realised that the job did not call for that level of ability.

If you see a job that you want to apply for advertised in the job centre or in an employment agency, the staff there will either arrange an interview for you or tell you how to apply if they think you are suitable for the job

If you have to telephone:

- Be prepared to explain why you want the job and what skills you have to offer.

- If you are using a public telephone use a phonecard so that your money doesn't run out in the middle of your call or if you are using your mobile 'phone make sure you have enough units available.

- Don't hang up if you hear an answering machine – leave your name and details of where you can be contacted.

If you have to write:

- You should say clearly what job you are applying for, where you saw it advertised and ask for an application form.

- Give three or four reasons why you should be considered for the job.

Keep a copy of your application form!

Preparing your CV

CV stands for **curriculum vitae**. The term is Latin. The dictionary definition says a CV is the course of one's life. Many companies and organisations ask for a CV when you apply for a job or you could send it to a company to see whether you are suitable for any job they may have. A CV is a way of telling an employer about yourself in a simple and easy to read way. The important thing about a CV is that it must be:

- Accurate – without even the smallest 'white lie'.
- Up-to-date.
- With no spelling or typing, or writing mistakes – always get someone else to check it for you before you send it out.

You will need to ask one or two people to act as referees on your CV – you should ask a teacher, a social worker, your doctor, or someone for whom you have worked before, people who know you reasonably well, and who you think will speak positively and honestly about you. They may be asked to comment on your character, and your suitability for the job you are applying for. Every time you give the names of the referees when applying for a job, you should tell the people concerned, giving brief details of the job you have applied for. Always keep a copy so you can:

- Read it before an interview.
- Up-date it when necessary.
- Use it as a help when filling in a job application form.

There are many ideas about the best way to write a CV. On page 110 is just one example.

 What is a person specification?

When some companies have a vacancy for a job they draw up and send out a **person specification** highlighting the qualities they are looking for in their employee. If this happens, you may need help with this application to show that you have the particular qualities – you may not think you have them nor be confident enough to say so: ask your carer to help.

Job interviews

Before going to an **interview** for a job you should:

- Find out what you can about the job and the company.
- Talk over with your social worker, your carer, keyworker or personal adviser, mentor or teacher why you want the job and what you can offer.
- Decide in advance what you are going to wear and get it ready. If you aren't sure what to wear, ask your carer. Wear something that is comfortable but smart.
- Make sure you know exactly where the interview will be and how long it will take you to get there, so that you arrive in good time.
- Look at the copy you have of your application form to remind yourself of what you have said.
- When you arrive say you have come for an interview and ask at the reception desk where you should go. You will be shown where to wait.

CURRICULUM VITAE

NAME
Samantha Brooks

AGE
15

DATE OF BIRTH
23rd June 1989

ADDRESS
26 St. John's Avenue
Fareham
Hampshire
PO25 1XX

TELEPHONE NUMBER
0123 0000

EDUCATION AND TRAINING
1999-2004: Ballharbour School

I will be taking the following exams in June:

Subject:	Type of Examination:
English	GCSE
Mathematics	GCSE
Geography	GCSE
Biology	GCSE
Music	GCSE

I have also gained my bronze life-saving award.

EMPLOYMENT AND WORK EXPERIENCE
I have worked in Newswell newsagents on Saturdays since November 1998.

INTERESTS
I enjoy badminton and swimming and I also help run the school aerobics club.
I am a member of the school choir and I play the piano to grade 3 standard.

REFEREES

Mrs. P. Green
Head of School
Ballharbour School
Smarts Lane
Fareham PO23 2YZ
Tel. 01234 567890

Mr. S. Singh
(Manager of Newswell)
42 Station Road
Portsmouth
PO1 1ZZ
Tel. 01987 65321

Figure 10.1: Example of curriculum vitae

At the interview

Below is a list of hints to give a young person who is going to an interview:

- Be friendly to everyone that you meet from the company but not too friendly.

- When you go in, look at the interviewer and shake their hand if they offer their hand to you. A handshake that is too bold may be considered a bit much, but a wet wishy one is worse! Only sit down when asked.

- Don't chew gum or smoke, even if offered a cigarette.

- Sit in a straight and upright (but relaxed) position and don't fidget.

- Think before you reply and then answer the question fully, not just 'yes' and 'no'.

- Be alert and interested. Sound positive and enthusiastic.

- At the end of the interview, thank the interviewer and say goodbye.

Typical interview questions:

- Why do you want to work for us?

- What have you got to offer?

- What were your favourite subjects at school?

- What are your long-term aims?

At the end of the interview you may be asked if you have any questions, so prepare some in advance. If you can't think of anything, just say 'I think you covered everything I need to know'. Before you leave try to find out when you will hear the result.

If there are two people interviewing you at the same time, speak to whoever asks you the question.

Getting an offer

After the interview you might get a **job offer** either by phone or in writing. If you are offered a job and you want to take it, write immediately saying thank you for the offer and how pleased you are to accept it. However, get someone to read any documents or contract before you sign them. If you decide not to accept the offer, write back and say so as soon as possible.

You may get asked to come back for another interview. This may be with the same interviewer or with somebody you have not met before.

Getting a rejection

You may be told, over the phone or in writing, that you didn't get the job. Ask the company why you were not successful. Think about the reasons why you were not chosen and learn from the experience, so that you are well prepared for the next interview you get.

Hearing nothing at all

If you have heard nothing within two weeks, telephone and ask whether a decision has been made.

Replying to a job offer

When you reply to an offer:

- Reply as soon as you can.
- Follow instructions e.g. telephone if it says to do so.
- Set out your reply correctly.
- Write neatly.
- Cover all the points mentioned.

Review sheet

It's a good idea to keep a record of the **job applications** you have made. For each application, you could include:

- name of company
- job title
- date of application
- date reply received
- action
- results
- comments

How to keep your job!

Once a young person has a job, the important thing is to help them keep it.

 When I start work, what do I need to know?

Many young people will have lived unsettled lives and the discipline and the stress of going to work will not come easy. Do you remember your first day at work? Talk it through with them and also remind them of such essentials as:

- Good time-keeping – not just at the start of the day but after breaks.
- Attendance: good attendance is a must, but if you **really are** too ill to go to work, either you should phone in or you must get someone else to explain the situation and say when you may be expected back.
- Asking if you don't understand – no-one minds repeating something but they will mind incorrect work.

- Everyone makes mistakes – own up promptly and provided mistakes don't happen too often no-one will mind too much, particularly for new staff.
- You will be the junior and may not be spoken to as you should – this is not right but may happen. 'Bite your tongue' and do not react except in extreme circumstances – think first, count to 10.

Many jobs, especially in the early days may be boring. Don't give up, as:

- If you stick at it you'll probably be given a better job when one is available.
- You'll actually feel quite pleased with yourself as well. It should give you confidence and self respect.
- It's easier to get another job when you're in a job than if you're unemployed.
- It will be a useful talking point at another interview.
- You'll probably get a reference from your first employer.

A young person who has had a disruptive childhood may need to try several jobs before settling into the right one for them. They will need all the help and encouragement you can give them.

 What if I think I'm being discriminated against?

At work young people may find they are victims of discrimination. They may need your help to handle this and to know their rights.

Discrimination in any form is not acceptable. There are also a variety of laws which make discrimination illegal – CAB, for example, will be able to give more information and also advise about making a claim if this is appropriate. You could speak to the person at work responsible for staff, often called the **personnel manager**, or a **union representative** if there is one.

Keeping up appearances

In most jobs, appearance and personal hygiene are important and many young people find looking clean, tidy and smart all the time difficult. Help them to understand that they are now representing their company and must create the right image. In practical ways help them to make sure they have room to hang their clothes properly, or to wash and iron them. Advise them on the best material to choose for any new clothes they buy or on their make-up, jewellery or hairstyle. The young person's social worker may be involved in some of this work.

Feeling isolated and lonely: support networks

If a young person feels isolated or lonely they could contact or visit any of those shown in Figure 10.2

	Samaritans	
	Carers	
Local after-care group		Old school friend
	Family and relatives	
		Other people who have been looked after
	Other people who have been helpful in the past	
Ex-teachers		Youth leader
	Local drop-in centres	
Community groups		
	Church/Temple/Mosque	

Who else might help?
Photocopy and fill in the other 'bricks' with any people you feel could give support.

Figure 10.2: Chart for support networks

What practical things would help?

There are lots of practical ways you can suggest to young people to help make the transition to independent living seem less daunting. Encourage them to:

- Keep an address book with names, addresses and telephone numbers of families, friends and any of the above.

- Swap addresses with friends.

- Let everyone know their new address if they move on.

- Give an address of someone who will know where they are and let other people know who it is. Someone may want to contact them.

What else might help?

Taking some positive action like:

- Doing something to help others.

- Going jogging, swimming or doing some other physical activity.

- Taking up a new hobby or sport.

- Joining a club or society.

- Learning a new skill.

- Changing the layout of a room, spring cleaning it or even decorating it.

- Drawing a new support chart.

Housing checklist

Many local authorities run courses to help young people prepare to leave care and others leave it to their carers to help them. Either way, a young person could go through the following checklist when they have found somewhere they think is suitable to live.

ACCOMMODATION CHECKLIST

Is it near work / college / shop / bank / buses / trains?	
Cost per month? .... **which equals cost per week?**	**Deposit?** .... **Get it back?**
Pay rent?	Weekly / monthly
What's included?	Rent / gas / electricity / rates / tv / 'phone / other
Notice to leave by you or landlord?	Weeks / months
Contract to sign?	Yes / No
Have you or someone else read it? **Checked it?**	Yes / No Yes / No
Rent book?	Yes / No (get it signed **every** time you pay rent)
Inventory (list of what's there)	Yes / No Checked correct? Yes / No
Does everything work and in condition stated?	Yes / No *If not, agree with the landlord who will get it repaired and how the repair is to be paid for. Don't sign anything until this is done.*
Read the meters?	Yes / No Agreed with landlord? Yes / No
Watch out for high rate meters that use money fast!	

Becoming independent

There are many practical aspects to becoming independent. Young people will settle much more easily if you can draw their attention to the kind of things they may face, what support they have, and who they are before they leave your care.

The aim of the checklist on the following pages is to find out what a young person knows and how ready they are for independence. Some young people may need your help to read it or fill it in. Others may flatly refuse. This may reflect their anxiety about becoming independent so they may need additional help and support. The checklist could also be used as a way of discussing how other young people would be better helped to prepare for their independence.

The answers to the questions should be not whether the young person **is able** to do these things but whether they **actually do** them. The questionnaire may be answered in one go, or in stages. The young person can go back and add or change things whenever they wish. It is not a test.

The areas covered are:

- Helping young people to build relationships with others.

- Helping young people to develop self-esteem and pride.

- Practical skills, financial skills and knowledge.

- Their future.

The checklist also asks what they think, as it is important for young people not just to have knowledge but to think about getting as much information and help as they can.

- Talk over the answers with them.

- Help them make a plan, with a time limit, of what help they would like.

It can be photocopied and used again by the same young person in a year or so or, when filled in, kept as a record for future use.

INDEPENDENCE CHECKLIST

Name ....

Date of birth ....

Foster carer or keyworker ....

Date completed 1st time ....

Dates changes made ....

A. Education or employment

1. Which of the following are you doing?

	where?	full-time	part-time
• school	....	❏	❏
• college	....	❏	❏
• further education	....	❏	❏
• work experience	....	❏	❏
• youth training	....	❏	❏
• work	....	❏	❏
• unemployed	....	❏	❏
• registered with careers office	....	❏	❏

2. Would you say that you attended the above

regularly ❏

more than half ❏

less than half ❏

3. Why do you think your attendance is the way you say it is?

....

....

....

....

→

B. Social contact

1. Do you attend, belong to or take part in one or more of the following?

	regularly	sometimes
• church/temple/mosque/synagogue	☐	☐
• local youth club	☐	☐
• sports club	☐	☐
• hobby or activity	☐	☐
• outdoor activity trips	☐	☐
• Duke of Edinburgh Award	☐	☐

what level and what activities? ....

....

• other ....

....

2. Is there any other outside event or place that you go to where you meet other people? (e.g. a disco, the town centre)   How often?

....

....

3. Where you can get a discount on leisure schemes in your area? ....

....

....

If you don't know, would you like to find out?   Yes ☐   No ☐

4. Do you have friends of your own age locally?   Yes ☐   No ☐

Do they visit you, or you them?   Yes ☐   No ☐

Have you stayed overnight at one another's homes?   Yes ☐   No ☐

Do you have any older friends?   Yes ☐   No ☐

Who? ....

→

C. Family

1. Which members of your family do you contact?

	by phone	how often	visit	how often
parents	❏	....	❏	....
brothers and sisters	❏	....	❏	....
step-parents	❏	....	❏	....
foster family	❏	....	❏	....

2. Do you know about your family history? Yes ❏ No ❏

3. What else would you like to know? ....
....

4. Where can you get this information? ....
....

5. Is there anyone you would like to contact or trace? ....
....

D. Achievements

1. What school or college qualifications have you got or are expecting to get?
....

2. What sports or hobby awards or certificates have you? ....
....

3. What other courses have you done (e.g. first aid)? ....
....

4. What personal ambition or resolution have you achieved in the last year?
....

5. What job interviews (including work experience) have you attended? ....
....

→

E. Taking part in making decisions about leaving care

1. Do you go to your group meetings? Yes ☐ No ☐

2. Do you attend your reviews? Yes ☐ No ☐

    (date of last one) ....

3. Where do you want to live when you leave?

    family ☐ friends ☐ foster carers ☐ supported lodgings ☐

    independent living units ☐ on you own ☐

4. Do you want to live locally or near your family if they live in a different area?

    ....

F. Practical skills

Reading, writing and maths

1. Which newspaper or magazine do you read? ....

		Yes	No	Would you like help?
2.	Do you understand job adverts in the paper?	☐	☐	Yes ☐
3.	Can you write a letter? (e.g. applying for a job?)	☐	☐	Yes ☐
4.	Have you got a CV (personal information sheet)?	☐	☐	Yes ☐
5.	Can you follow a recipe/instructions on packets?	☐	☐	Yes ☐
6.	Can you add up a shopping list?	☐	☐	Yes ☐

7. Which of the following bills have you seen?

    food ☐ clothes ☐ electric ☐ gas ☐ water ☐ rates ☐

    TV licence ☐ council tax ☐ telephone ☐

    rent (as part of a written agreement). ☐

    Do you understand all of them? If not, would you like some help?

    Yes ☐ No ☐

→

Shopping

1. How do you buy your clothes?

   Adult buys them ❑   They pay, you choose ❑

   You shop independently ❑   Mail order ❑

2. How often and where do you go food shopping? ....

   ....

3. Have you been food shopping on your own?   Yes ❑   No ❑

4. Do you choose some of the menus?   Yes ❑   No ❑

5. Have you made a budget for a week's shopping?   Yes ❑   No ❑

Preparing food and cooking

1. Are you able to use a cooker safely?

   Gas?   Yes ❑   No ❑

   Electric?   Yes ❑   No ❑

2. Do you help prepare or cook meals?   Yes ❑   No ❑

   How often? ....

3. What hot meals do you cook for yourself, and when?.......................................

   ....

4. Do you plan your meals so that you get a balanced diet?

   Yes ❑   No ❑   Need help ❑

5. Do you know how long food keeps in a fridge or freezer?

   Yes ❑   No ❑   Need help ❑

6. Do you lay the table and wash up?   Yes ❑   No ❑

→

Household

Can you?:	Yes		Yes
wire a plug	❑	read a meter	❑
change a light bulb or fuse	❑	check on electricity, water or gas bill	❑
unblock a sink	❑	use a calculator	❑
turn a water stop-cock off	❑	measure length, weight and fluid	❑
sewn on a button	❑	do simple first aid	❑
do simple mending of clothes	❑	mend a puncture on a bike	❑

G. Managing money

1. What is your weekly income? pocket money £............... earnings £...............

2. Do you save any? Yes ❑ No ❑ How? ....

3. How much do you pay towards your keep each week?   £...............

4. What do you spend the rest on? ....
....

5. Are you given any other cash by the adults (e.g. for travel, leisure)?
Yes ❑ No ❑

6. If you borrow, how you do pay back? ....
....

7. What do you spend money on that you wish that you didn't? ....
....

Would you like help to stop? Yes ❑ No ❑

➜

H. Health and health education

1. How do you arrange to see your doctor or dentist? ....

....

2. If you move, do you know how to register with a new doctor?

Yes ❑   No ❑

3. Have you been given enough information on the following?

sex education	Yes ❑ No ❑	alcohol	Yes ❑ No ❑
contraception	Yes ❑ No ❑	smoking	Yes ❑ No ❑
HIV/AIDS	Yes ❑ No ❑	diet	Yes ❑ No ❑
legal and illegal drugs	Yes ❑ No ❑	fitness	Yes ❑ No ❑

Would you like more information? Yes ❑   No ❑

About ....

I. Privacy

1. Have you keys for the front door?   Yes ❑   No ❑

for your room?   Yes ❑   No ❑

2. Do you have your own bedroom?   Yes ❑   No ❑

3. Do you have a safe and secure place to keep valuables? Yes ❑   No ❑

4. Do you have somewhere that you consider to be private? Yes ❑   No ❑

5. Are you able to be in and be alone?   Yes ❑   No ❑

J. General information and rights

1. Are you a member of the library?   Yes ❑   No ❑

Do you use it?   Yes ❑   No ❑

2. Do you know what the telephone numbers of these agencies are?

police station   ....

dept. of social security   ....

housing offices   ....

employment service (job centre)   ....

doctors' surgery   ....

Samaritans   ....

citizens advice bureau   ....

→

3. Who do you complain to if things are not right? ....

....

4. What is your social worker's name, address and phone number? ....

....

5. What should you do if stopped by the police or arrested? ....

....

6. How do you get free legal advice? ....

....

   Would you like help? Yes ❑   No ❑

7. How do you get in touch with an appropriate adult? ....

....

   Would you like help? Yes ❑   No ❑

8. Where are your birth certificate ....

                     national insurance number ....

                     national health card ....

9. At what age does the law allow you to:

smoke	....	have sex	....
drink alcohol	....	vote	....
get married	....	appear in adult court	....

10. Have you been given advice on:

	Yes	No	Do you need help?
how to apply for a job or use the job centre	❑	❑	❑
your rights	❑	❑	❑
racism	❑	❑	❑
religion	❑	❑	❑
housing	❑	❑	❑
social security	❑	❑	❑

11. When you are 16 you can put your name on the electoral register. You will then be able to vote when you are 18. Do you need help to get on the register? Yes ❑   No ❑

→

K. **Feeling isolated** →

    1.   Where do you go for help if you really feel bad about something or someone or just feel lonely? ....

....

    2.   Have you got an address book with names and telephone numbers in?

        Yes ☐   No ☐

    3.   What ideas do you have on how to overcome loneliness? ....

....

....

....

    4.   If there is a crisis in your life, such as breaking up with your longstanding boy or girl friend, what would you do? ....

....

....

    5.   How do you go about making new friends? ....

....

....

L. **Nationality and ethnicity**

    1.   What is your nationality? ....

    2.   If you are not British, does anything need to be done to sort out your immigration, citizenship and nationality status? ....

....

    3.   Do you have all the documents needed for future dealings over passport, immigration etc.? ....

→

4. Who can help? ....

5. Have you got an up-to-date passport? Yes ☐   No ☐

6. Who will be able to sign the form to support your application for a passport?

   ....

7. Which ethnic group do you come from? ....

8. If you come from a minority ethnic group do you need help to meet more people from the same background? Yes ☐   No ☐

Is there anything else that has not been asked that you think is important?

....

....

....

....

....

....

Your carer and social worker may be able to help you with some of this information. You could also try your local library or citizen's advice bureau.

(Adapted from *Leaving Care from Therapeutic Communities*, unpublished thesis by James Cathcart, University of Southampton, 1992).

Section 11
Legal terms

Introduction: the law and being looked after

Most young people will never attend court in their life. Many will never have a court order that refers to them. Unfortunately, this is not true for young people who are looked after. Going to court or having a court order placed on them can be very distressing for young people. One way of helping a young person to better understand the situation is to give them as much information as possible. This chapter sets out what many of the **legal terms** mean but it does not cover **criminal law**.

Being accommodated

What does **being accommodated** mean? This is a technical term where there is no **care order**. It means that social services provides somewhere for a young person to live if:

- There is no-one who has parental responsibility for them.
- They have been lost, abandoned or have been thrown out of their home.
- The person caring for them cannot provide accommodation or care at present.
- They might come to harm if they go on living where they are.
- They might suffer ill-treatment from another person.
- The police or the court have asked social services to provide accommodation for them.

Court orders and The Children Acts

Court orders which affect children or young people are made under The Children Act 1989, The Children (Scotland) Act 1995 or The Children (Northern Ireland) Order 1995. Court orders are only made if something can be achieved by that order, which will be for the good of the young person, and the court thinks it is better than making no order. You may need to explain to the young person the reasons for going to court, the decisions the court could make, and to help the young person prepare for going to court. If there is a court order then it will automatically end when a young person is 18 unless it is stopped by the court earlier. Someone will be appointed by the court to talk about the young person's wishes and feelings (usually called a **children's guardian**, **guardian ad litem**, **curator ad litem** or **safeguarder**) and a **solicitor** will be appointed to represent them. Both these people should ensure that the young person's view is heard. An **interpreter** may also be necessary if the young person's main language is not English.

If a young person is being accommodated by the local authority, there is no court order.

The court must:

- Consider what is best for the young person.
- Make sure that whatever is to happen, happens as soon as possible.
- See that nothing changes unless it is best for the young person.

They must consider:

- What the young person wants.
- Any needs they may have.
- What the effect will be on them of any changes.
- Their age, sex, background or anything else that might be appropriate.
- Any problems there may have been in the past or are likely to be in future.
- The ability of the parents, guardians or carers to meet those needs.

On the next pages there is a brief explanation about the various orders that might be imposed.

Court orders: a summary of what they mean

Child assessment order

A **child assessment order** is an order made by the court stating that the parent or those with parental responsibility must take the young person to the specified place e.g. doctor, hospital, health centre, so the young person may be assessed. The order is made:

- In the case of the parents or those responsible refusing to co-operate.
- When the local authority or authorised person thinks the young person might be in danger of significant harm but the young person is in no immediate danger.

If, after looking at all the evidence, immediate action is needed, then an **emergency protection order** will be made and the young person may be asked to have a **medical examination**, either physical or psychiatric. They may refuse provided they fully understand what is going on.

Emergency protection order

An **emergency protection order** is made if the court has reason to believe that:

- The young person will come to significant harm if they continue to live where they are, or if they are removed from where they are staying.
- The young person is are suffering significant harm and their parents/carers will not allow doctors or social workers to see them.

The order cannot be stopped or challenged within the first 72 hours. After that it may be challenged in court. It can last up to eight days and then be extended for a further seven days.

The young person may be asked to have a medical examination, either physical or psychiatric, but they may refuse provided they fully understand what is going on. Child assessment and the emergency protection orders may be made at the same time.

Exclusion order (Scotland only)

An **exclusion order** is made to allow the alleged abuser to be removed from the home, rather than the child.

Interim care order (ICO)

An **interim care order** is sometimes made, lasting for not more than eight weeks, to give the court time to collect more information. Further ICOs can be made which will last up to four weeks each.

The young person may be asked to have a medical examination either physical or psychiatric but they may refuse provided they fully understand.

Care order

A **care order** is made by the court and states that social services must look after the young person and provide somewhere for them to live. A care order gives social services **parental responsibility**. Young people must be encouraged to see their family and friends unless the court states otherwise.

A care order is made if the court thinks the young person might be suffering significant harm or likely to suffer significant harm and the care they are being given is not what a parent should give, or that the young person is beyond their parents' control. A care order will only be made if making the order will help the young person.

The care order stands until one or more of these events happens:
- the young person is 18
- the young person is adopted
- a supervision or residence order is made
- the court stops the order
- the young person, their parents, social services or the person with parental responsibility asks the court to stop the order and the court agrees

Contact order

A **contact order** is an order made by the court stating who can keep in touch with the young person. It might be their birth parents, brothers and sisters, grandparents or anyone who is important to them. You should allow these people to visit, stay with them, write to them or speak on the phone according to the rules set up by the court. The order can be made by the court when they are asked to by one or more of the following:
- the young person concerned or someone close to them
- their parent or guardian
- their foster carers if they have been living with them for three years

In fact anyone may apply.

A contact order lasts until the young person is 16 years old or until the court agrees it is no longer necessary. In exceptional circumstances it may last until the young person is 18 years old, if the court thinks it is necessary.

Interim supervision order

Sometimes an **interim order** is made for up to eight weeks so that more information can be collected. Another may be issued for a further four weeks if necessary.

Supervision order

A **supervision order** is made when a supervisor, usually from social services, is appointed to advise, help and befriend a young person and to make sure any other conditions the court set are carried out. It is made when social services are worried that the young person may be suffering harm or is likely to suffer harm because the care they are getting is not what it should be, or that they are beyond their parents control.

It usually lasts for one year but no longer than three years and not after the young person is 18 years. It can be stopped if a care order is made or if any of the interested parties apply in court and the court agrees.

Residence order

A **residence order** is a court order stating:

- where the young person must live
- with whom the young person must live
- whether that person will be given parental responsibility, if they haven't got it already

The young person cannot leave the country for more than a month (nor can they change their surname) without the written permission from whoever has parental responsibility, or from the court. Any interested party can apply to have a residence order stopped at any time. It usually lasts until the young person is 16 but occasionally until they are 18.

Prohibited steps order

This is an order made by the court stating that certain things cannot happen without the court's permission. The court won't make a **prohibited steps order** if there is a better way of sorting things out or if the young person is already under a care order. It lasts until the young person is 16, unless there are exceptional reasons for extending it.

Specific issue order

A **specific issue order** is an order made by the court when there is a disagreement about how the young person should be brought up. It might be about schooling, or religion, or health care etc. It means that the court will decide, after consulting others, what should be done and how it should be done in the interests of the young person. A specific issue order won't be made if there is a better way to sort things out, or if there is a care order.

It usually lasts until the young person is 16 years old. The young person's parents or guardian, anyone who has a residence order for them, or the person who applied for the first order to be made, may apply to have it stopped.

family assistance order

The **family assistance order** is sometimes made after the young person's parents get divorced. Someone will be appointed to advise, help and befriend the young person, their family, the person caring for them, or the person named on a contact order. They must be allowed to visit the young person regularly and be told of any change of address.

It lasts for no longer than six months unless a new order is made.

Adoption

There are over half a million adopted people living in Britain today. Young people aged 12-18 are not adopted very often. Adoption is usually for the younger child, but sometimes young people in the 12-18 age group may want to know about adoption. An **adoption order** is a court order: the court decides whether an adoption can go ahead.

 What happens in adoption?

The family the young person lives with may want to adopt them, or the young person may ask their family to adopt them. In all cases the social worker will talk it through with everyone concerned and fill in the necessary forms. The family then apply to the court and an investigation takes place to look at all the circumstances and information, and then make recommendations to the court.

 What does being 'freed for adoption' mean?

It means that the young person has been released from their birth parent's responsibility in preparation for being adopted but must be looked after by social services until the adoption is finalised. It also means that they are **protected** and no-one can do anything until the court decides whether or not an adoption can go through.

 What is an adoption panel?

It is a group of between five and ten people, including someone from social services, teachers, health visitors, someone from the adoption agency, who meet to make sure:

- The adoption is in the young person's best interest.
- The family is suitable to adopt.
- The young person is suitable for that family.

How long will it take and what will be different?

There is no set time and it will be different every time but if a young person is 'freed' it will be quicker.

 ## What about my name?

Most adopted young people take the name of their new family.

 ## How will I compare to other children in the family?

A young person who has been adopted will get the same rights and status as any other children in that family:

- You will gain extra family such as grandparents.

- You won't have a social worker (you can still see them but it is most unusual).

- You won't have reviews.

- You won't normally see your birth parents but you may have contact with them if you want to.

- You will get a new birth certificate with an adoption entry on it. When you are 18 you can apply to see your original birth certificate.

The court decides whether an adoption can go ahead and the new parents will be sent a letter explaining the adoption.

 ## What if I want more information?

The local social services office may be able to help but you can also contact the relevant organisations, such as BAAF, listed at the end of this book. In certain circumstances local authorities can provide help to families who want to adopt but are unable to because they are on a low income.

Special guardianship

A **special guardianship order** will enable certain people such as family or close family friends to apply to the court for permission to care for a child. Although parents will remain the child's parents and will retain parental responsibility, their ability to exercise their rights as parents will be limited by the terms of the special guardianship order.

Guardianship and wardship

Some young people may have a guardian and do not understand what it means. The following might help you explain things.

 ## What is a guardian?

A guardian is a person who is given **full parental responsibility** for a young person because their parents have died. The guardian will have the same responsibilities that parents would have had.

 ## Who can appoint a guardian?

- Anyone with parental responsibility.
- Any other guardian.
- A court.

 ## When does guardianship stop?

- When the young person is 16.
- When the court orders it to stop.
- When either the young person or someone with parental responsibility applies to the court to have it stopped and the court agrees it is in the best interest of the young person.

 ## What is wardship?

Wardship gives the court continuing responsibility for the young person. The Children Act has reduced the use of wardship. It has diminished because prohibited steps orders, specific issue orders and residence orders have largely taken the place of wardship. Wardship cannot be used when there is a care order.

 ## What is inherent jurisdiction?

Occasionally the court will use **inherent jurisdiction** in order to protect a young person. What this means is that the court has retained certain powers to enable it to take action if the need arises and it is in the best interests of the young person. Local authorities can only use inherent jurisdiction in exceptional circumstances, when The Children Act does not enable the young person to be protected from significant harm.

Leaving care

The leaving care legislation has been provided to ensure that young people who leave the care of the local authority:

- Should be prepared and ready to leave care.
- Have been assessed and appropriate plans made for their future.
- Have in place personal support for when they have left care.
- Are aware of their entitlements and have in place adequate financial arrangements including funding for further and higher education.

Records

Many young people see the records social services keep on them as a cause for concern. They do not like people writing things about them that they are not allowed to see. They also do not like the fact that the records are sometimes left lying around for everyone else to see. They feel they should be kept locked away with only certain people being allowed to read them. The following questions look at how records should be kept in the light of the Children Acts.

 What records do social services keep on me?

They may keep four sets of records on every young person. These include:

1. a straightforward list of who is accommodated
2. case records
3. management records
4. *Looking After Children: Assessment and Action Records* (most local authorities are now using these)

 What is on these records?

1. The list of who is accommodated shows:

- the real names of the young person as well as the name they wish to be known by
- where they are staying
- what happens
- their telephone number
- their date of birth
- the name of their social worker

In most authorities this will be kept on the computer and updated either by the social worker or by the administrative assistant.

2. Case records (as well as the information listed above) should show:

- details of their family
- their plan
- any reports written about them such as court reports, health, home study etc
- review documents
- details of court orders
- details of arrangements made for contact with their family
- any special arrangements
- any documents used to find out more about the young person such as psychological or court reports

The young person may also ask to have other documents such as certificates or school reports kept with this information.

 Who else keeps the records?

Children's homes keep records about the young person and these are usually very similar to the case records.

Foster carers are sometimes given only brief written documents about a young person. This depends on the practice of the local authority. However, it is essential for them to keep their own records for future reference. This could be in the form of a foster carer's diary, listing events, illness, accidents as well as specific details about the young person. If the foster carer is involved with the young person's court case or accompanies the young person to court they may be given a copy of the court order.

3. Management records
These will be the same as case records except that details of carers will be included.

4. Looking After Children: Assessment and Action Records (or other assessment documents used with young people)
These are a set of questions covering:

- health
- education
- identity
- family and social relationships
- social presentations
- emotional and behavioural development
- self-care skills

Young people should help complete these records. They are used to make sure every step possible is being taken to try to ensure the young person is developing to the best of their ability. At the back of these records there is a summary of what action needs to be taken and by whom.

Can I see my records?

Every young person has the **right to see** their records if they wish. There must be a very good reason for anyone saying no. Some records are written by other agencies and cannot be made available to them. When a young person sees their records for the first time, what is written may come as quite a shock and they may need help to cope with this.

What do I have to do to see them?

Some local authorities have introduced systems to make sure only certain people see the records. This, unfortunately, has sometimes made it difficult for the young people to see them. If the young person wants to see them, you will have to find out what the system is and help them follow it.

Who else can see them?

All these records are **confidential** with only authorised staff able to see them. The case records and the management records should be held in a safe place so that only those people shown below may see them:

- the young person's social worker, superiors and the young person
- a government inspector
- a children's guardian, curator ad litem, safeguarder

How long will the records be kept?

The computer records are kept until the young person is 23, or if they die before that, for five years after their death. Case records must be kept for 75 years from the date they were started; or for 15 years after the young person's death if they die before they are 18 years old.

It is a good idea for young people to keep their own records such as in a daily diary as it will assist them in recalling events accurately and may prove helpful in expressing their feelings. The records should, of course, be confidential to the young person unless they choose to share them with anyone.

Parental responsibility

By law there are certain things parents should and should not do when bringing up a young person. They must ensure that a young person gets correct medical treatment, full education, and that their physical, moral and religious needs are met.

Who has parental responsibility?

If a young person's father and mother were married to each other when they were born, or have since married, they both automatically have parental responsibility.

 ## What if my parents didn't get married?

Only the mother has parental responsibility automatically. If the father was not married to the mother he can do one of the following:
- Apply to the court for parental responsibility.
- Draw up a formal agreement with their mother which must be registered with the court.
- Ask to be made their guardian or to be granted a residence order by the court.

There are proposed changes to bring parental responsibility rules in line with other legislation affecting the status of parents, to ensure it adequately reflects modern social attitudes and conditions. It may be that in the future there will be an automatic link between biological parentage and parental responsibility, so that all fathers will have parental responsibility for their children, whatever their marital status at the time of the child's birth.

 ## Who else can get parental responsibility?

- The parents can delegate it to someone else, but they won't lose it themselves.
- An adoptive parent automatically gets parental responsibility.
- A guardian.
- A special guardian.
- The person with whom the young person is living if a residence order is made.
- The local authority gets it if a care order or emergency protection order is made.

 ## How long does parental responsibility last?

Until a young person is 18, but a court order may cancel it before then.

Changing your name

Many young people want to be called a different name for many reasons such as:
- Bad memories of their father or mother, or of their stepfather or stepmother
- To try to create a new identity.
- Because it's easier to be known by the name of the rest of the family – this often happens when young people are fostered.
- Just because they simply don't like the name they've got.

I want to change my name. Can I?

Yes. Whatever the reason you can do this simply by asking other people to call you by any name you wish. If you want to change your name for legal purposes then you can do so by deed poll or statutory declaration. In either case this means going to a solicitor. This proves to others that you have changed your name. There will be a charge for this work, and you should find out what it is before instructing the solicitor to proceed.

 ## What happens if I am on a care order or residence order?

Young people can change their first name at any time, but to change their surname they must have the written permission of whoever has parental responsibility for them or the court.

 ## Why should I bother to go to court to change my name?

As we said earlier there is nothing to stop anyone changing their name but if a young person decides that the change is permanent then it is better to do it formally. If they don't, it may cause problems later in life, for example, if they want to join the armed forces. The citizens advice bureau should be able to give more details.

Section 12
Useful contacts, telephone numbers and addresses

BAAF (British Association for Adoption and Fostering) promotes public understanding of adoption and fostering; develops high standards of practice amongst child care and other professionals; provides high quality training tailored to meet specific needs; acts as an independent voice in the field of child care to inform and influence policy makers.

BAAF, Skyline House, 200 Union Street, London, SE1 0LY. Tel: 020 7493 2000

Fostering Network (previously NFCA) has, over the past 28 years, taken the lead in raising standards for the 40,000 UK children and young people in foster care. It is committed to seeing that their concerns are given a voice and ensuring services are developed to meet their needs. With a membership of 20,000, including 99% of all local authorities and 18,000 foster families, the organisation is involved in foster care from the children to the very highest point of policy making. The services it provides include dedicated workers for young people, advice, mediation, information and consultancy as well as an extensive training and publications programme.

Fostering Network, 87 Blackfriars Road, London, SE1 8HA. Tel: 020 7620 6400

Northern Ireland: 216 Belmont Road, Belfast BT4 2AT. Tel: 028 9067 3441

Scotland: 2nd floor, Ingram House, 227 Ingram Street, Glasgow G1 1DA.
Tel: 0141 204 1400

The Family Rights Group offers an advice line for parents, relatives and carers who have children and young people in contact with social service departments.

Family Rights Group, The Print House, 18 Ashwin Street, London, E8 3DL.
Tel: 020 7923 2628

The National Children's Bureau carries out research, and influences policy and practice on matters relating to young people and families. They may be able to answer general questions or pass you on to someone who can.

National Children's Bureau, 8 Wakely Street, London, EC1V 7QE. Tel: 020 7843 6000

Voices of the Child in Care exists to empower young people to speak out for improvement in the quality of their lives by providing information, advice and advocacy; raising awareness of children's rights; campaigning for changes in law, policy and practice; supporting the active participation of young people; delivering high quality services; ensuring equality of opportunity and anti-discriminatory practice; and providing a link for people and agencies who aspire to good childcare practice.

Voices of the Child in Care, 4 Pride Court, 80 White Lion Street, London, N1 9PF. Tel: 020 7833 5792

Voices from Care (Cymru) offers training, advocacy, befriending, support and advice on leaving care, benefits, housing, drugs and rights. It was set up by, and for, young people who are, or have been, looked after in Wales. All the advice and support workers have personally experienced the care system themselves as children or young people.

Voices from Care (Cymru), 25 Windsor Place, Cardiff CF10 3BZ. Tel: 029 2039 8214

Who Cares? Offers a practical service for young people on health; education; counselling; employment and information. They communicate with 20,000 young people through the Who Cares? magazine published quarterly.

Who Cares? Trust, Kemp House, 152-160 City Road, London, EC1V 2NP. Tel: 020 7251 3117

Selected reading

Ahmad, W.U. (Ed.) (1993) *Race and Health in Contemporary Britain*, Open University.

Aldgate, J. and Simmonds, J. (Eds.) (1988) *Direct Work with Children*, Batsford, BAAF.

BAAF (1987-90) *Range of Workbooks for Use with Children and Young People*, BAAF.

BAAF (1991) *Children who Foster*, Training materials, BAAF.

Barn, R. (1993) *Black Children in the Public Care System*, Batsford, BAAF.

Batty, D. (1993) *HIV Infection and Children in Need*, BAAF.

Batty, D. and Bayley, N. (1984) *In Touch with Children*, Training pack, BAAF.

Bower, S. and Bower, G. H. (1991) *Asserting Yourself: A Practical Guide for the Positive Change*, Addison & Wesley.

Braithwaite, A. (1981) *When Uncle Bob Died*, Dinosaur.

Braithwaite, A. (1989) *I Have Cancer*, Dinosaur.

Bremner, J. and Hillin, A. (1994) *Sexuality, Young People and Care*, Lyme Regis, Russell House Publishing.

Buchanan, A., Wheal, A., Walker, D., Macdonald, S. and Coker, R. (1993) *Answering Back, Report by Young People Being Looked After Under the Children Act 1989*, Department of Social Work Studies, University of Southampton.

Bullock, R., Little, M. and Millham, S. (1993) *Going Home: The Return of Children Separated from their Families*, Dartmouth.

Burningham, J. (1984) *Grandpa*, Cape.

Cathcart, J. (1992) *Leaving Care from Therapeutic Communities*, unpublished thesis, University of Southampton.

Collins, D., Tank, M. and Basith, A. (1993) *Concise Guides to Customs of Minority Ethnic Religions*, Arena.

Couldrick, A. (1991) *When Your Mum or Dad Has Cancer*, Sobell.

Damani, P., Churcher, P., Birch, J., Khaira, A. and Warren, V. (1995) *Play with Confidence: A Training Pack for Those Wishing to Introduce Children to Multiracial Britain*.

Daws, D. (1993) *Through the Night, Helping Parents and Sleeping Infants*, Free Association Books.

Department for Education (1994) *Special Educational Needs: A Guide for Parents*, DFE.

DoH (1989) *The Care of Children: Principals and Practice*, HMSO.

DoH (1990) *An Introduction to the Children Act*, HMSO.

DoH (1990) *Protecting Children: A Guide for Social Workers Undertaking a Comprehensive Assessment*, HMSO.

DoH (1991) *Patterns and Outcomes in Care in Child Placement*, HMSO.

DoH (1991) *The Children Act 1989: Range of Leaflets and Guides for Parents and Young People*, HMSO.

DoH (1991) *The Children Act 1989, Guidance and Regulations, Volumes 1- 9*, HMSO.

DoH (1991) *The Children Act 1989, Guidance and Regulations, Index*, HMSO.

DoH (1991) *Working Together Under the Children Act 1989, A Guide to Arrangements for Inter-agency Co-operation for the Protection of Children from Abuse*, HMSO.

DoH (1993) *Looking After Children, Assessment and Action Records*, HMSO.

DoH (1999) *National Standards in Foster Care*, The Stationery Office.

Duckley, D., Orritt, B. and Thelwell, D. (1990) *Going into Care*, The Children's Society.

Family Rights Group (1991) *The Children Act 1989, Working in Partnership with Families*, HMSO.

Gambe, D., Gomes, J., Kapur, V., Rangel, M. and Stubbs, P. (1992) *Improving Practice with Children and Families*, CCETSW.

Hampshire County Council (1991) *My Guidebook*, Ashford Open Learning.

Heegaard, M. (1991) *When Someone Has a Very Serious Illness*, Woodland.

Heegaard, M. (1991) *When Someone Very Special Dies*, Woodland.

HMSO (1989) *Access to Personal Files (Social Services), Regulations*, HMSO.

HMSO (1989) *The Children Act*, HMSO.

Jeynes, L. (1993) *Would You be a Foster Carer?* Linda Jeynes.

Karmi, G. (Ed.) (1996) *The Ethnic Health Fact File*, The Health and Ethnicity Programme.

Lindon, J. (1993) *Child Development from Birth to Eight: A Practical Focus*, National Children's Bureau.

McCartt Hess, P. and Ohman Proch, K. (1993) *Contact: Managing Visits to Children Looked After Away from Home*, BAAF.

Millham, S., Bullock, R., Hosie, K. and Little, M. (1986) *Lost in Care. The Problem of Maintaining Links Between Children in Care and Their Families*, Gower.

MNDA (1993) *When Someone Special Has Motor Neurone Disease*, MNDA.

National Children's Bureau (1997) *Religion, Ethnicity, Sex Education – Exploring the Issues*. NCB.

National Foster Care Association (1999) *Report and Recommendations of the UK Joint Working Party on Foster Care*, NFCA.

National Foster Care Association (1999) *UK National Standards for Foster Care*, NFCA.

National Foster Care Association (1999) *Code of Practice on the Recruitment, Assessment, Approval, Training, Management and Support of Foster Carers*, NFCA.

National Foster Care Association, *A range of leaflets on many areas of foster care*, NFCA.

Neuberger, J. (1987) *Caring for Dying People of Different Faiths*, Lisa Sainsbury.

Newell, P. (1991) *The UN Convention and Children's Rights in the UK*, National Children's Bureau.

NSPCC (1997) *Protect Your Child: A Guide about Child Abuse for Parents*, NSPCC.

Parents Aid (1991) *A Guide for Families: Your Child and Social Services*, Parents Aid.

PHAB (undated) *Teachers' Notes on Physical Disability*, Hampshire Project, PHAB.

Porteous, M.A. (1985) *Porteous Problem Checklist and Inventory of Adolescent Problems*, NFER-Nelson.

Schulz, C.M. (1990) *Why, Charlie Brown, Why?* Ravette.

Simmonds, P. (1981) *Fred*, Puffin.

Stickney, D. (1990) *Waterbugs and Dragonflies*, Mowbray.

Thomson, R. (Ed.) (1993) *Religion, Ethnicity Sex Education: Expoloring the Issues*, Sex Education Forum, National Children's Bureau.

Triselioti, J. and Marsh, P. (1993) *Prevention and Re-unification*, Batsford, BAAF.

United Nations (1989) *The Convention on the Rights of the Child*, UNICEF.

Varley, S. (1985) *Badger's Parting Gifts*, Collins.

Wessex Regional Health Authority (1992) *Eat Well, Be Well*, Wessex Regional Health Authority.

West, S. (1993) *Open Sez Me, The Magic of Pleasant Discoveries*. Spring, Summer, Autumn, Winter.

Wheal, A. with Buchanan, A. (1994) *Answers, You and the Young people in Your Care*, Pavilion Publishing.